CONTENTS

RAMESSES THE GREAT
WARRIOR AND BUILDER

Bernadette Menu

THAMES AND HUDSON

The fame of the Egyptian pharaoh Ramesses II (sometimes spelled Ramses) was extraordinary during his own time, and remained legendary throughout classical antiquity. In the present day he once more enjoys a renewed popularity, due to the charisma of his personality, the splendor and imperial influence of his long reign, the prosperity he brought to Egypt, and the enduring monuments that he bestowed upon posterity.

CHAPTER 1

THE ORIGINS OF A REIGN

The official Egyptian calendar began anew with the first year of each pharaoh's reign. Because the length of reigns is uncertain, the year in which Ramesses II (left) gained the throne occurred in either 1304, 1290, or 1279 BC. This last date is the most accepted. Right: the goddess Hathor, in the form of a cow, protects the king.

Archaeological records and inscriptions bearing the name of Ramesses II are plentiful, as are extant works of art from his time. In the history of ancient Egypt, therefore, the period of his rule is relatively familiar to modern scholars. In recent decades numerous excellent popular and technical books and exhibition catalogues on Ramesses II have been published, and it is now possible to reexamine his reign in light of new information about his institutional, international, socioeconomic, and cultural achievements.

Who was Ramesses II?

From these abundant documents, the portrait of Ramesses that emerges is complex and multifaceted. Born to privilege, probably in the late 14th century BC (c. 1304?), he was blessed with exceptional longevity, was spouse and lover of the most beautiful women of his time, husband to four of his own daughters, and father to some 100 children. A member of the established royal family, he came to the throne of a land already quite stable politically. He was a pious ruler and bold general: wall paintings and reliefs depict him launching into battle, raising his great war cry after offering a prayer to the god Amun. He is often shown fighting alone, or almost alone, against a multitude.

An enthusiastic patron of art and architecture, this wealthy and dynamic king sponsored massive public building programs, including many of the grand monuments that still draw innumerable visitors to Egypt. The splendid temples at Abu Simbel in Upper Egypt are principally his, as are those at Luxor (Egyptian Thebes), on the banks of the Nile.

A notable legislator and diplomat, he was adept at organizing and administrating the vast empire he had founded. His ambitions were expansionist and colonial, and during his reign Egypt extended its borders and hegemony considerably. To the east of the Nile Delta he built up the luxurious capital (founded by his father) that bore his name: Piramesse.

The reign of Ramesses II is noted for the grand scale of its architectural program, vestiges of which dot the Nile Valley. Below: his temple at Abu Simbel.

According to Egyptian religious tradition, the pharaoh was half-divine, a demiurge gifted with the miraculous ability to discover precious water sources. He was the son of Re, sun god and creator, and the nurturing father of his people, like the god Osiris. Ramesses had red hair and was called the "redhead," signifying that he was also a disciple of the cult of the storm god, Set.

Quite simply, Ramesses II was the pharaoh *par excellence,* a king deeply aware of his great lineage and his place in history, and devoted to sustaining the continuity of the monarchy. He was driven by a sense of royal destiny and a desire to surpass all his predecessors in reputation, including his own father, Seti I, whom he

"You devised your plans even while you were in the womb in your role as the infant prince; the affairs of the Two Lands were referred to you while you were a young boy, still wearing your child's curls. Not a monument was erected that had not been under your authority."

Inscription on the Quban Stele

Opposite: Ramesses II.

admired. It was said that the Seven Hathors, equivalent to our good fairies, watched over the cradle of Ramesses II and forged an extraordinary destiny for him.

He saw to it that his exploits as a ruler and a man were widely recorded, so that they might be remembered forever, and his fame be eternal. A skilled propagandist, he well understood the value of art in documenting earthly glory. Yet three thousand years later we are free to judge him not only by his commissioned artworks, but by the records of his acts and laws, the opinions of those who came after him, and the views of the peoples he ruled and conquered. Ramesses II seems truly to have possessed the physical, intellectual, and moral qualities of a leader of stature. He dominated the Near East for much of the 13th century BC, and long after his death his presence cast a shadow from the Fifth Cataract of the Nile to the banks of the Euphrates, even long after the glory of Egypt had begun to decline.

B elow: Thutmose III (1479–1425 BC), conqueror of the rival empire of Mitanni (or Nahrin), was named as a symbolic hero in innumerable amulet-scarabs and is sometimes considered the greatest pharaoh. The imperial structures with which he endowed Egypt were further developed by Amenhotep III and Ramesses II.

The legacy of the 18th Dynasty

The reign of Ramesses II marks the culmination of the imperial efforts of two earlier pharaohs: Thutmose III (reigned 1479–1425 BC), conqueror of Syria–Palestine, and Amenhotep III (reigned

c. 1390–1352 BC), who carried Egypt to the height of power and brilliance and whose opulent court typified the splendor of the 18th Dynasty. This dynasty was the first in the period known as the New Kingdom. Amenhotep's son was the "heretic" pharaoh Akhenaten (reigned 1352–1336 BC), who attempted to alter Egyptian religion, introducing worship of the solar disk, Aten. He established a short-lived capital at Tell el-Amarna

O pposite: the vizier Pa-Ramessu, later pharaoh Ramesses I. In dedicating a chapel to his father at Abydos, Seti I expressed his gratitude: "His lessons were like a rampart for my heart."

Horemheb, last king of the 18th Dynasty, was the founder of the 19th. The historians of Ramesses II's time described him as the direct successor of Amenhotep III, attributing to him the years of the intervening reigns of the discredited rulers Akhenaten, Tutankhamun, and Ay. Their purpose was to erase the memory of the Amarna period. Nevertheless, Horemheb's tomb at Saqqara contains marvelous reliefs (left) whose delicate style is quite similar to that of the artists at Tell el-Amarna.

and his reign, known as the Amarna period, was marked by dramatic innovations in art. Egypt at this time had already attained great power, controlling broad territories, but Akhenaten's digression into mysticism isolated the country from the international scene's political contests and military alliances.

After Akhenaten, the 18th Dynasty foundered in struggles over the succession. Following the death of the young king Tutankhamun, generals in the Egyptian army assumed power and the title. The last of these was Horemheb, final pharaoh of the 18th Dynasty.

The advent of the 19th Dynasty

The 19th Dynasty was founded by Ramesses I and brought to fame by his three immediate successors, Seti I, Ramesses II, and Merenptah. In all, 11 pharaohs of the 19th and 20th dynasties bore the name Ramesses, so that this phase of the New Kingdom is called the Ramesside period.

Pa-Ramessu, a general and vizier under

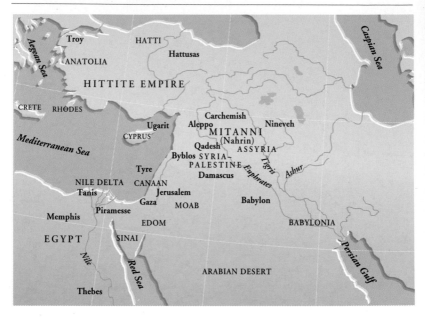

Horemheb, received the titles "chief of archers, quarter-master of horses, chief of seals, driver of His Majesty, royal emissary to all foreign lands, royal scribe, commander of the army of the Master of the Two Lands, High Priest of all the gods, lieutenant to His Majesty in both Upper and Lower Egypt, commander of the mouths of the Nile, prince and governor of the city." He was already old when he came to the throne under the name of Ramesses I, and reigned only briefly, but his legacy was assured by his son Seti, and grandson Ramesses II.

Of military and plebeian origins, the new dynasty rose to power through a dominating will, and at once set out to restore the empire of Thutmose III and Amenhotep III.

At the crossroads of three continents

Egypt is situated strategically at the northeast corner of Africa, linked to western Asia by the Sinai Peninsula; to the Mediterranean, and thence to Europe, by the Nile Delta; and to Subsaharan Africa by the great river itself. Its Mediterranean coast faces the large islands of Cyprus

The Near East in the time of Ramesses II.

The land of Egypt fell naturally into two distinct regions: to the north, the wide marshy river delta, and to the south and along the mid-course of the Nile, a long narrow fertile valley surrounded by desert and mountains. To keep Upper (southern) and Lower (northern) Egypt unified was a constant worry, as records of numerous royal rituals and political measures attest.

and Crete, where much of European civilization was born. The Syrian–Palestinian corridor and the Sinai, the Mediterranean and its islands, the Red Sea, the Nile Valley that runs south to the great confluence of the Atbara and Blue Nile Rivers—all these constituted avenues for the transport of peoples, goods, techniques, wealth, and ideas. Even the arid desert that has stretched across it breadth since prehistoric times is crisscrossed with ancient trade routes. New research in the past 30 years has exposed the richness of this commerce and

The key to Egypt's great agricultural fertility has always been the annual flooding of the Nile, which deposited rich silt on both shores from the dawn of history until the construction, in the 20th century AD, of the Aswan Dam. This periodic flood, deified under the name of Hapy,

negated the old image of an isolated Egypt.

Egyptian territory was clearly described by its four cardinal points: to the north lay the wetlands of the Delta and the Mediterranean shore; to the south, the first cataracts of the Nile; to the east, the ribs of the Arabic mountain range beyond the Red Sea; and to the west, the Libyan plateau. In this perfect rectangle, two axes are distinctly evident: the course of the sun from east to west between the two mountainous horizons, and the long line of the Nile, flowing from south to north. As had been the convention in ancient China, the Egyptians in the age of the pyramids added a fifth cardinal point: the

punctuated the seasons, dictated the calendar, and marked the landscape with sharp contrasts: the green farmlands of the Nile Valley and the bordering arid desert, ocher dust and black earth, the world of the dead and the world of the living. The land itself reveals a fundamental duality composed of complementary elements.

center, which completes and perfects the geometric balance.

From Syria to Sudan, Egyptian hegemony

From the most ancient times, ties existed between Nubia (now Sudan), Egypt, and the area known as Syria–Palestine. Between Africa and Asia, Egypt played a stabilizing role, both disseminating its own culture and assimilating influences from its neighbors. The pharaonic dynasties endured for almost three millennia, an almost unimaginably long period of basic political continuity. Even so, Egyptian rule was defined as much by tensions and

The Near East empire formed by the four pharaohs named Thutmose and the four Amenhoteps comprised a cluster of more or less autonomous cities and states under Egyptian supervision. The colonizer sent army garrisons and a governor who collected tribute. The pharaohs built temples to the national Egyptian divinities: to Amun at Gaza and to Amun or Ptah at Jerusalem. The semiautonomous princes of Syria–Palestine sent their children to Egypt to be educated. Nubia, on the other hand, was administered directly, as an Egyptian province. Below: the temple of Wadi es-Sebua, in modern Sudan, dedicated to Re and the deified Ramesses.

ruptures, expansions, divisions, and reunifications, as by persistence. It was often called the "Two Lands," meaning Upper Egypt (including Nubia) and Lower Egypt (including the Delta region).

To the west, Egypt made no important territorial conquests, save for very early on, when it linked a string of oases that runs from north to south through what is known today as the Western Desert. Military activities there were mainly defensive, guarding against invading Libyan tribes. To this end the pharaohs built high fortresses along the western arm of the Nile Delta and along the seacoast west of what is now Alexandria. When Ramesses II gained the throne, his land was well established from Syria to Sudan. To consolidate his hold, he established the new capital of Piramesse (Pi- [or Per-] Ramesses, the "House of Ramesses") in Lower Egypt, in the eastern Nile Delta at the border of Djahi, an area comprising Canaan and regions to the north. In Upper Egypt he created an administrative seat in Nubia. Throughout the realm he built a network of temples.

A hymn to Amun dating from the reign of Ramesses II proclaims: "Three are all the gods, Amun, Re, Ptah who have no equals. / His name is concealed as Amun; his face is that of Re; his body, that of Ptah. / Their cities, in the Country, have been established for all of eternity; Thebes, Heliopolis, Memphis are destined in perpetuity. / When a message is sent from heaven, it is heard in Heliopolis, repeated in Memphis for the God with the Beautiful Face [Ptah]; / registered in the writings of Thoth [the divine scribe] for the city of Amun, that being their domain. / The [divine] plans were given in response to Thebes."
Above: Amun, at right, embraces Ramesses II.
Opposite: the god Ptah.

The political expansion of Egypt into Syria was founded on the stability of Nubia, source of great riches. This province was administered by the "Royal Sons of Kush," also known as the viceroys of Nubia. The most eminent of these, Setau, served under Ramesses II. Between the First and Third Cataracts of the Nile, Ramesses II constructed a series of temples consecrated to the three primary divinities of the empire. These were, from north to south, Beit el-Wali, dedicated to Amun-Re; Gerf Husein, to the house of Ptah associated with Ramesses; Derr, to the house of Re, master of the sky (where Ramesses II established a cult associated with Re-Harakhte and Ptah); Abu Simbel, a large complex that comprises the great temple where Ramesses was revered together with the three great gods and the small temple of Hathor, dedicated to Queen Nefertari; Aksha, where the statue of the pharaoh was worshiped together with Amun and Re; and Amara West, dedicated to Amun-Re, as well as to other gods of the Cataract, of which Ramesses himself was one. Here, from left to right, are the statues of Ptah, Amun, Ramesses II, and Re in the sanctuary of the great temple at Abu Simbel.

The gods of the empire

The land of Egypt housed a multitude of gods, some quite local, but all honored in official documents. Preeminent among these are what may be termed the national gods—Amun, Re, and Ptah, venerated by Seti I and his son Ramesses II. The connection between religion and dynastic politics was an intricate one, which the 19th Dynasty exploited fully.

Amun, the god of Thebes in Upper Egypt, had been declared a dynastic god by the rulers of the old Middle Kingdom. Re, whose cult was based in the holy city of Heliopolis (near modern Cairo), was the sun god, the creator of the world. Ptah, patron of the ancient city of Memphis, was a god-craftsman, also endowed with the power of creation. Numerous other gods occupied the Egyptian pantheon, among them bovine Hathor, daughter of Re, a fertility figure; Horus, the falcon-god who governed divine kingship; his mother, Isis, wife and sister of Osiris, god of death and afterlife; the ram-god Khnum, who dwelt at Elephantine and fashioned humans from clay on his potter's wheel; Neith of Sais, the ancient, primordial goddess; Thoth, god of writing, sciences, and the law, who resided in Hermopolis.

The three tutelary gods of the kingdom, Amun, Re, and Ptah, represented the demiurgic forces from which the king was born, and which legitimated his rule. For this reason, Amun of Thebes, Re of Heliopolis, and Ptah of Memphis (in order of importance, followed by all other Egyptian gods) were the focus of intense ritual activity. Vast domains were dedicated to them, comprising agricultural lands and their farmers, pasturage and cattle, and fishing concessions. Under Ramesses, the wealth of these religious holdings grew, in particular that of Amun.

In predynastic times, Set and Horus contested the place of supreme god of the kingdom. The preference of the 19th Dynasty for Set was converted in following epochs into a hostility to this god. Left: a statue of Set transformed into Amun, his long ears having been cropped and replaced by goat horns.

The arch of the great rock stele of Nauri in Nubia bears an image of Seti I offering a statuette of Maat (the goddess of cosmic order and justice) to Amun, Re, and Ptah. The three gods are guaranteeing Seti's allocation of possessions and privileges to the god Osiris at Abydos; Maat, as intermediary, confirms the new redistribution of land. Beneath this scene an inscription records a decree (128 lines long) that explains how these great land grants are to benefit the cult of Osiris in Seti's funerary temple at Abydos, called the temple "of a million years."

A great innovation of the reign of Ramesses II—whose precedent was set under Amenhotep III—was the establishment of a cult honoring the royal person and his statues: a worship of the living sovereign himself, assimilated to divine principles.

Brothers, enemies

Together with his birth name, every Middle Kingdom pharaoh bore a set of epithets, called royal titularies, that described his godhood and kingship. One of the five royal titularies of Seti I was "Repeating the Births," referring to both the inauguration of the cycle of creation by Osiris, god of resurrection, and to the renewal of the kingdom brought about by the new dynasty.

Paradoxically, the god Set, brother and enemy of Osiris and an antagonist of Horus (heir to the divine throne of the gods), was also raised to the rank of dynastic god by the Ramessides—indeed, the name Seti signifies an adherence to Set. For beast-headed Set, lord of confusion, represented the battle against evil. Placed in the bow of the boat of Re, he warded off the forces of chaos incarnated in the serpent-god Apophis. Set was the god of necessary violence, of the disorder that permits a

The sun god was the universal demiurge, self-created. As such he has many names: the name Re refers to the star; Khepri is the rising sun, charged with potentiality; Atum is the setting sun, signifying accomplishment. From Re was born the so-called Ennead, the company of nine gods that included Shu (air), Tefnut (humidity), Geb (earth), and Nut (sky). The four children of Nut were Osiris, Isis, Set, and Nephthys. Re, ruler of the world, and Osiris, ruler of the afterlife, were the two "great" gods.

Left: Ramesses II stands before Re, enthroned, in falcon form and with a solar-disk headdress, as Re-Harakhte (Horus). Below: horned Osiris grasps the royal insignia,

a *heka* scepter and a *nekhakha* flail, signifying government and protection. Egyptian foundation myths assert that the kingdom originally belonged to Osiris, who passed it to his son Horus, who in turn bequeathed it to the pharaoh.

return to order, the god of sudden rains, of the tempests that precede the calm. Set was the favored god of the Hyksos (a Greek corruption of the name *heka khaswt*, "rulers of foreign lands"), Palestinians who had ruled in Egypt from the mid-17th century BC to the mid-16th, until they were overthrown by Ahmose, founder of the 18th Dynasty.

Set was the god of the borders between Egypt and Asia, a model for the many foreign gods who were invited to join the Egyptian pantheon. Most often associated with the Canaanite god Baal, he played an important role in the religious vector between the two regions.

Ramesses II, whose mummy still reveals his red hair, was marked from birth as a "companion of Set," whose symbolic color was the nefarious and dangerous red (whereas Osiris, for example, was associated with the black color of the Nile's precious fertile silt).

Senenmut (fl. c. 1470 BC), architect and favorite of Queen Hatshepsut of the 18th Dynasty, placed an astronomical ceiling in his tomb. The theme was taken up by Seti I in his own tomb, the largest and most splendid of the dozens that dot the Valley of the Kings. Animals and figures symbolize stars and constellations.

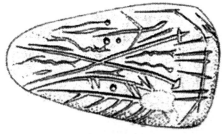

Seti and Ramesses made efforts to restore the god Set to a position of honor. They invoked a myth now thought to have a shared Syrian–Egyptian origin, and which dates back to the 8th millennium BC. Excavations in the village of Jerf el-Ahmar, on the banks of the Euphrates 60 miles (100 km) east of Aleppo, have unearthed some interesting little engraved stones from this ancient period (below and

By reestablishing an adherence to the cult of Set and founding their capital upon the ruins of that of the Hyksos, at the border of Egypt and Canaan, first Seti and then Ramesses declared a policy of territorial expansion and cultural assimilation.

In the official phrase used in some of the inscriptions of Ramesses II, Set and Horus were the "Two Masters," the co-proprietary gods of Egypt who conferred the kingdom upon their earthly representative, born of divine seed.

A grandiose vision of the royal office

In the pharaonic system, the sovereign was an exceptional being, predestined,

left). On two of them a pair of animals is clearly distinguishable. A quadruped (a fore-shadowing of Set?) chases a bird of prey with spread wings (an early form of the falcon Horus?) in a tangle of weapons.

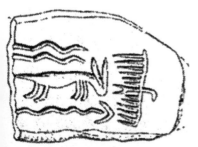

elect, and born of the gods to pursue their creative work on earth. He (or she) was omniscient, privy to nature's secrets and an adept of cosmic forces. To be ruler meant to command both the normal cycles of the astrological and agricultural calendars and extraordinary and astounding events.

This supernatural vision of the royal purpose had very ancient origins and was reinforced by an imperial proclamation of Amenhotep III. The concept was further glorified in the reign of Ramesses II.

The founding documents

The first pharaoh in Egyptian history was Narmer, who founded the state in c. 3100 BC and promulgated a body of laws preserved in three great sculptural reliefs: the so-called Palette of Narmer and two gigantic maceheads, one known as the Macehead of King Scorpion, the other as the Macehead of Narmer. (A palette was originally a slate or schist tablet upon which powdered paint was ground.) Through the ages these documents were preserved by successive pharaohs in the temple at Hierakonpolis, where archaeologists later found them. They—and perhaps others now lost— form a veritable written constitution, expressed in symbolic scenes.

Egypt in the late Neolithic era was converting from a hunting-and-gathering economy to one based on agriculture, characterized by animal and plant domestication. This impelled a new socioeconomic organization, with new political structures. The earlier loose confederation of territories under a principal chief was replaced by an autocratic monarchy ruling by divine right. Narmer

Below: on the Narmer Macehead, the king wears the White Crown when in a role of power and the Red Crown in ritual contexts. These crowns later came to symbolize Upper and Lower Egypt, respectively.

embarked upon the pacification and ordering of the country, aided by provincial chiefs (represented in the graven documents by their insignia). He then drafted the basic principles that governed the pharaonic monarchy for the next three millennia.

The Macehead of King Scorpion bears three registers of scenes, in which we note the coexistence of gods and humans. At the top, ethnic and territorial ensigns of the local gods are depicted; before the king (oversized to indicate his status) stands a group of four human standard bearers. These figures also appear on the other macehead and the Palette.

This macehead documents the new organization of agriculture. The king, wearing a tall miter called the White Crown, stands in a dynamic posture. Armed with a hoc, he makes a gesture of opening the earth in order to exploit it, both by technology (irrigation, planting, sowing, and harvesting) and by the performance of fertility rites. The Macehead of Narmer depicts the regulation of animal breeding. The king, wearing the Red Crown, a flat cap topped with a spiral shaft, is seated under a canopy, counting livestock as ritual fertility ceremonies take place. Here the insignia of the local gods have disappeared; only the four standard bearers remain to define royal power. The Palette, the founding charter of the kingdom, uses both image-script (symbolic images) to express its rules and the first instance of hieroglyphics.

The Palette of Narmer does not commemorate the unification of Egypt, which had already been achieved by Narmer's predecessors in the predynastic period (also called Dynasty 0). Its aim was to define the absolute and sacred power of the sovereign, as well as the geographic extent of the kingdom. Below: the four standard-bearers who proclaim the law, a detail from the palette. These figures also appear on the Maceheads of Narmer and (left) King Scorpion.

L eft: the administrative and religious roles of the king are depicted on the recto of the Narmer Palette, in a narrative scene at top, and symbolic form at bottom. (At center are two fantastic beasts whose meaning is obscure.) At the upper left corner the sovereign wears the Red Crown, symbolizing his governance. Preceding him in royal procession are the four standard-bearers, whose poles support symbols associated with royalty and power. These are, from left to right: the royal placenta, representing the king before his birth (which is symbolically situated in the east, like that of the sun); the dog Khentimentiu, guardian god of the western necropolises, also called the dead and deified king (whose life terminates in immortality in the west, like the sun); and the two falcons, personifying royal authority over Upper and Lower Egypt (to the south and north). Thus the four cardinal points of the compass are also represented. (Indeed, the number 4 itself evokes the compass points.) The scene proclaims the king's absolute power; he integrates the forces of

nature along the two axes that describe his land: the course of the sun from east to west (as the king moves from the womb to eternal life); and the course of the Nile, from south to north (as the king wields jurisdiction over Upper and Lower Egypt). The standard-bearers serve as both the definers of the territory and the bearers of the symbols that translate the concept of the permanence of the kingdom.

Left: the verso of the Narmer Palette depicts the king as a warrior, bringing down an enemy. This scene was often reproduced by later pharaohs, especially Ramesses II. The king wears the White Crown, representing power. Through *sekhem* (god-given power), he expels *isfet*, evil forces (enemies, misery, chaos, injustice, etc.). Through *heka* (magical) government, he brings *maat*—the antithesis of *isfet*: victory, prosperity, order, and justice. This nexus of symbolically represented concepts of government is found, with infinite variations and developments, in the official documents of all the pharaohs, and particularly in those of Ramesses II.

The expanding empire

The domination of Egypt by the Palestinian Hyksos had created a sense of humiliation and of dispossession. When Ahmose (founder of the 18th Dynasty) expelled them from their capital in the eastern Delta of the Nile and pursued them all the way to Palestine, the impulse to create a comprehensive empire was born. From that point on, a sequence of pharaohs conquered more and more land, extending Egypt from Asia to Nubia. Of these, the undisputed master was Thutmose III, who, after the peaceful reign of his aunt Hatshepsut, expanded the borders of the country south to the Fifth Cataract of the Nile and east to the banks of the Euphrates River. The cost was great, for Egypt suffered considerable destruction in the course of his wars. Yet, once Nubia

The so-called Colossi of Memnon— actually two huge statues of Amenhotep III—owe their name to an ancient Greek legend. At sunrise, as the stone warmed, it shifted, causing one of the figures to emit a melodious sound that was interpreted as the voice of the mythical king Memnon, greeting his mother, the Dawn. These statues had originally stood before the funerary temple of Amenhotep III, which has long since vanished.

was colonized and the cities and kingdoms of the Near East subjugated, the pharaohs were able to create a highly profitable confederated political system, in which duties were paid to the pharaoh. Egypt thus attained unequaled wealth and an incomparable sphere of influence.

The five scarabs of Amenhotep

The great pharaoh Amenhotep III wrote an imperial constitution for all the territories under his rule. This was published in the form of five large stone scarabs incised with texts, each reproduced in thousands of copies and distributed from Sudan to Asia. These stone documents proclaimed to the known world the authority of the pharaoh, his power, the extent of his territory, and the solidity of his alliances.

The scarabs were a set. Each acclaimed an aspect of the monarchy, and each was linked, by the inscription on its flat side, with imperial motifs: the Scarab of Marriage defined the empire geographically ("from Karoy to Nahrin," that is, from Gebel Barkal in Nubia to the banks of the Euphrates) and affirmed its authority and legitimacy. The Scarab of Gilukhepa asserted the prestige associated with a royal alliance in the name of Tiy, the Mitannian wife of Amenhotep III. The Scarabs of the Lion Hunt and the Bull Hunt, which celebrated specific events, also referred to the important concept of *sekhem*, royal power. Similarly, the Scarab of the Lake denoted another key royal concept, that of *heka*, the magical power by which government achieves *maat*, or divine order.

Amenhotep III, like all New Kingdom pharaohs, had a fivefold royal titulary (a set of royal titles) that also represented a sort of political platform. The constitutional foundation of the empire, condensed in the five names of the king, is encapsulated in five concepts:

Below: the pharaoh Amenhotep III, author of the five scarabs. The scarab pictogram is a hieroglyphic word: *kheper,* meaning "to become, to exist, to appear." Khepri is a name for the creator-god associated with the rising sun. Scarabs are thus linked to a solar symbolism and express arrival, existence, and the future—all ideas contained in the imperial concept. Cosmopolitan, opulent, and refined, the reign of Amenhotep III profoundly impressed Ramesses II.

1) victory; 2) organization and ordering of the country; 3) power;
4) influence and authority over
a vast, defined territory;
5) dynastic bloodlines and
the prestige associated with
them. These five names follow
a set formula, and may be
correlated with the inscriptions that appear on the five
scarabs. They are:
• The name Horus, "the
victorious bull who appears
in Maat," connecting the
pharaoh's kingship with the
divine rule of the falcon god and
expressing victory. It is associated
with the Scarab of the Bull Hunt.
The king assumes the brutal
strength of the bull to bring down
his adversaries.
• The name He of the Two Ladies,
"he who confirms the laws and
brings peace to the Two Lands,"
placing the king under the goddesses
of Upper and Lower Egypt (represented by the cobra symbol of the
North and the vulture of the South). This
is linked to the Scarab of the Lake.
• The name Horus of Gold, "the Most
Valiant One, who struck down the
Asians," is associated with the
Scarab of the Lion Hunt. Valor
is the feature of the lion, and
on the lion statues of Soleb
Amenhotep is referred to as
"the Lion of Sovereigns."
• The name King of Upper
and Lower Egypt, Nebmaatre,
or "Re is lord of *maat*." This is
the throne name, establishing
territorial sovereignty, and may be

The titulary of
Amenhotep III is
represented on the head
of each of his five scarabs,
as is a reference to his
wife, Queen Tiy (left),
who exercised consid-
erable power, sharing her
husband's ritual and
diplomatic functions.
Below and opposite: the
inaccurately named
Scarab of Marriage, also
called the Scarab of Tiy,
bears the first article of
the imperial constitu-
tion proclaimed by
Amenhotep III. It is not
dated, since its purpose is
to affirm the enduring,
undying power and
legitimacy of the empire.

"That Horus may live: the victorious bull who appears in Maat [personification of *maat*, divine order]; He of the Two Ladies: he who confirms the laws and brings peace to the Two Lands; Horus of God [or "Conqueror of Set"]: the Most Valiant One, who struck down the Asians; King of Upper and Lower Egypt ["Re is lord of *maat*"]; Son of Re ["Amun is satisfied"]. Sovereign of Thebes, may he live! And the great royal wife, Tiy, may she live! The name of his father is Yuya; the name of his mother is Tuyu. She is the wife of a powerful king, whose frontier to the south stretches as far as Karoy, and whose frontier to the north is the land of Nahrin." These phrases are precise statements of sovereignty and power, legitimacy through marriage ties, and the definition of the realm from the Fifth Cataract of the Nile in Nubia to Mitanni.

identified with the Scarab of Marriage.
• The name Son of Re, Amenhotep, or "Amun is satisfied." This is the pharaoh's birth name, or nomen, and is linked with the Scarab of Gilukhepa.

Ramesses II adopted these elements and exploited them to their utmost, expressing them with grandeur in his vast public works. An inscription on the temple at Abu Simbel in Nubia defined the territory of his hegemony from north to south and from east to west, within which, he declared, all indigenous populations were able to move freely.

The 18th Dynasty, which set the terms of the 19th, faced numerous crises of succession, due to the absence of a direct male line of descent. The accession of Horemheb, who founded the line of Ramesses, was a matter not solely of his strength of character and loyalty to the state, but also of the existence of a son and grandson whose energy and robust health promised many years of stable government. These brilliant heirs were a notable asset.

CHAPTER 2
AN INITIATION TO POWER

In the third year of his reign, Ramesses II (left) supplemented his first name with Usermaatre Setepenre. Right: from the age of 21 his name was spelled Ramessu, as in this sculptural rebus at Tanis, which uses three-dimensional hieroglyphic figures, Ra (Re, the sun), Mes (the child), Su (the bulrush) seated under the protection of the god Hurun, in hawk form.

Ramesses I, founder of the dynasty, reigned for only one year and four months. Just as Geb, god of the earth, had placed his son Osiris on the throne and subsequently appointed his grandson Horus as heir, Ramesses I named his son Seti, to be followed by his grandson Ramesses, to reign over Egypt. He left them a country imbued with a new confidence in its strength, and the records of the kings of the 18th Dynasty to act as models. The most impressive of these were Ahmose the Founder, the

L eft: a portrait of the heretic ruler Akhenaten, in whose reign only the solar disk, Aten, was worshiped. This prepared the way for Ramesses II to appropriate to himself the attributes of the Creator, and to claim that the pharaoh, like Aten, was the source of all life. A hymn proclaims: "When you lie down on the western horizon, / the universe is plunged into shadows, as if dead. / Men sleep in their chambers, their heads shrouded, / And no one of them can see his future. / All the posses- sions they keep under their heads could be stolen, / They would sense it not at all! / All the lions have left their dens, / And all the reptiles are biting. / This is the darkness of an oven, / And the world lists in the silence. / For its creator rests on his horizon."

kings Thutmose I and II, and especially Thutmose III, the first three kings Amenhotep, and Horemheb the Restorer. Others of the previous dynasty were negative models, deeply abhorred for their failure to serve the imperial ideal (notably in military terms). These included the female pharaoh Hatshepsut, Tutankhamun and his followers, and above all Akhenaten the heretic, whose philosophical and religious pursuits led him to neglect the empire. Subsequent rulers reviled these

Left: this sequence of royal cartouches from the temple of Ramesses II at Abydos lists (from left to right) Ramesses II; Seti I, his father; Ramesses I, his grandfather. These are followed by the ancestors chosen by Ramesses II: Horemheb, preceded by Amenhotep III, Thutmose IV,

figures and, where possible, obliterated their names and images from the historical record.

Seti I, father of Ramesses II

Seti I was already well into his thirties when he acceded to the throne. His wife was Tuyu, daughter of a patrician military family (her father carried the title Lieutenant General of the Charioteers).

The new pharaoh had a reputation as a solid and devout man, a valiant warrior, and a good administrator. He dedicated monuments of sublime beauty to the gods, of which the temple at Abydos, decorated with splendid reliefs, remains a testament to the consummate artistry of his court. Here both the gods and the pharaonic ancestors were honored, for the sanctuary contained a famous list enumerating (selectively) the kings of Egypt from the founder

Amenhotep II, et al. Ignored in this ancestry is the Amarna period, during which both religion and the economy were destabilized and the traditional gods were evicted, their possessions confiscated.

Left: Seti I, father of Ramesses II; above: his mother, Tuyu, in a portrait found in her tomb. All extant effigies of her were endowed by her son, who thus demonstrated his filial piety.

of the 1st Dynasty to the ruling pharaoh. Seti restored
the temple of Set at Avaris in the eastern Delta and
constructed a sumptuous palace nearby. This was the
germ of the new city that his son Ramesses II was to
develop into the great capital Piramesse.

Seti concentrated many architectural works at Thebes,
on both sides of the Nile. On the left (west) bank he
established his funerary temple at Gourna and an
immense and magnificent tomb in the Valley of the
Kings; on the right bank he continued construction on

Below: a 19th-century
AD print illustrates
the funerary temple of
Seti I at Gourna, which
was completed by
Ramesses II. A sanctuary
to Ramesses I, founder
of the dynasty, is conse-
crated there.

Right: the vast
hypostyle hall of the

the hypostyle hall (a large court with many columns)
of the great temple at Karnak. Seti I also left his mark
on the two other religious capitals of Memphis and
Heliopolis, and his name is associated with a number of
sites in Nubia, Middle Egypt (el-Ashmunein), Sinai, and
Wadi Hammamat (east of Koptos), where great mines
and quarries were situated.

Seti developed gold mines in Nubia and in the
mountains to the south and southeast. In his decree at
the temple of Kanais in Wadi Mia (east of Edfu), he
set forth a gold-based monetary policy, which was
further amplified in the reign of his son Ramesses II.

temple at Karnak was
begun by Amenhotep III
and Horemheb and
continued under Seti I
and Ramesses II. It is
immense: 58,190 square
feet (5,406 meters),
supported by 134 gigantic
columns. On the north
wall are depicted the
Asian campaigns of Seti I
in bas relief.

Seti's territorial conquests

Seti pursued the effort of reconquest initiated by his father and by Horemheb. An inscription on the north exterior wall of the hypostyle hall at Karnak relates his military expeditions in Asia. A notable enterprise was his advance into Retenu, a region that extends from the Nile Delta to the Litani, a river in Lebanon that borders the Bekaa plains and flows into the Mediterranean north of Tyre. There, he claimed victory over the Hittites, the Amorites, and the Tehenu, a people of Libyan origin.

Under Amenhotep IV and Tutankhamun, Mitanni had been crushed by Hatti (the Hittite Kingdom in Anatolia), which shifted the balance of powers in the Near East northward. Once Egypt reconquered Canaan, Amurru (in modern Lebanon), Syria (the Damascus region), and the Phoenician coastal cities alternately passed from Hittite to Egyptian control, playing the indispensable role of counterbalances.

In probably the eighth year of his reign Seti I fought a campaign to pacify Nubia and recapture the water sources that led to the country of Irem, west of the Dongola reach of the Nile. He was probably assisted by Amenemopet, the viceroy of Kush, royal delegate and administrator of Nubia.

The crowning of Ramesses II

According to a stele in Quban, Seti's son Ramesses was already chief of the army at the age of 10. He probably ascended the throne in 1279 (a date still contested), and remained there for almost 67 years. Though historians long believed that there had been a regency shared by father and son, the idea has now been generally dismissed as inconsistent with the ideological and political concepts of the founding charters, which established a sun monarchy, divine, personal, and unique. Ramesses II was lieutenant

Below: a bas relief of the prince as a young man.

Left: a coronation scene of Ramesses II from the temple at Abu Simbel. Set and Horus place the Double Crown (the Red Crown combined with the White) on the king's head, but Horus alone wears the *pschent* headdress and confers divinity on him. In another coronation scene, at Karnak, the king, flanked by the Two Goddesses, receives the White Crown from the hands of Horus and the Red from the hands of Thoth. These crowns were the insignia of

power; the king is sometimes depicted wearing other headdresses whose purpose was liturgical.

Above: a Nubian prisoner.

and heir apparent to his father, who taught him the responsibilities of kingship and bestowed upon him several royal honors and attributes. Ramesses's great dedicatory inscription at Abydos recounts the moment when Seti transmitted the kingdom to his son: "When my father appeared to the people, when I was a child in his arms, he said to my subjects, 'Crown him king so that I may see his accomplishments while I still live!' "

Seti I reigned for less than 15 years and his son Ramesses gained the kingdom at about age 25. It was his goal to continue what his father had begun: leading the empire to its greatest stature and wealth.

The royal titulary of Ramesses

Following tradition, Ramesses's fivefold titulary pronounced his government policy, as guided by

imperial ideology. The five names follow the established formula, so that all but the last, personal names are essentially the same epithets as were used by previous pharaohs. The five are:
• Horus, mighty bull, beloved of Maat.
• He of the Two Ladies, protector of Egypt, conqueror of foreign lands.
• Horus of Gold, rich in years, great in victories.
• King of Upper and Lower Egypt, Usermaatre Setepenre, Strong is the *maat* of Re, or Re is the strength of Maat.
• Son of Re, Ramesses-Meryamun, "Born of Re, beloved of Amun."

These last two names, more or less equivalent to a given and surname, were enclosed together in Ramesses's cartouche. A cartouche is an elliptical symbol that might be considered the king's signature. Cartouches were sets of hieroglyphics within an oval line, an encircling, protective rope emblem, and were used for seals and as identification marks.

The canonical five names were inscribed on monuments and documents, together with the epithets that explain their significance—for example, on the obelisk of Luxor, now in the Place de la Concorde in Paris. In general, these names refer to two categories of power and government: *heka,* intended to bring *maat* (including organizational and ritual duties and the construction of monuments), and *sekhem,* concerned with wars and the administration of the realm, whose purpose was to drive back *isfet.*

"Horus: Victorious bull, beloved of Maat, king as dearly beloved as Atum, monarch son of Amun, beautiful throughout all of universal time. / King of Upper and Lower Egypt: Usermaatre Setepenre. / Son of Re: Ramesses-Meryamun. / As long as the skies shall exist, your monuments shall exist, your name shall exist, firm as the skies. / King of Upper and Lower Egypt: Usermaatre Setepenre. / Son of Re: Ramesses-Meryamun, blessed with life."

Inscription on the Place de la Concorde obelisk

L eft: a papyrus inscription lists the titulary of Ramesses II; below: cartouches on a vase with his first and second names.

Ramesses conducted the funeral of his father at Thebes and then himself led the lavish ceremonies of the great Festival of Opet, in which the god Amun, his wife, the goddess Mut, and their son Khons traveled in procession from Karnak to Luxor in sparkling golden barques bedecked with flowers, amid the cheers of a

During Ramesses's reign, the festivals of Opet, of the god Min, and of the Valley were especially important. In the Festival of the Valley, the god Amun traveled in his golden barque in a proces-

jubilant population. The reign began under favorable auspices.

The royal family

Ramesses II had two great royal wives, Isetnofret and the well-loved Nefertari, both of whom bore his legitimate heirs. He also contracted two diplomatic marriages with Hittite princesses and, following Egyptian dynastic tradition, married four of his daughters. One of these, who had the Asian name Bant-Anat, "daughter of the goddess Anat," was Isetnofret's child. Many of his numerous children (at least 50 sons and as many daughters) seem to have become titled and wealthy

sion to the Ramesseum, where he spoke to Ramesses: "Oh, my dearly beloved son, my heart is filled with joy because of the love you hold for me...I shall proclaim, for you, your victories over foreign lands; look, I place the South, like the North and the West and the East, under your authority."
Above: a painting depicts the Festival of Opet, in which the god Khons is carried in his barque.

officials in his administration. This was a policy inaugurated by his grandfather and continued by his father.

Numerous royal princes who might have been heir to Ramesses died before their father. The 13th son, Merenptah, was probably 60 years old when he ascended to the throne upon the king's death in 1213. A famous son by Isetnofret, Khaemwaset I, is often referred to as the archaeologist prince. He lived at Memphis

Left: a monumental portrait of Ramesses II in the temple of Amun at Karnak. His daughter and wife, the queen Bant-Anat, is depicted in small scale, emblematically. Statues of Ramesses often show him with his children, especially the prince-heirs Amunherkhepeshef, Ramesses, and Khaemwaset, as well as two daughters whom he married: Bant-Anat and Meritamun.

From a very early age, the sons of Ramesses shared the pharaoh's military and hunting

as high priest of the god Ptah, who was greatly venerated by Ramesses II. A historian, he studied the old texts preserved there and restored many already ancient monuments whose inscriptions were becoming illegible, reviving the memory and records of past pharaohs. He

exploits. Above: Ramesses and his eldest son, Amunherkhepeshef, hunt a wild bull. Hunting was sport and combat training, but it also assumed symbolic significance: the king, master of wild animals, assimilated the beasts' physical force.

also apparently organized royal ceremonies (jubilees, or *sed* festivals) and was associated with the cult of the bull-god Apis, an animal form of the god Ptah.

Luminaries of the reign

We know the names, and something of the careers, of many of the officials who supported the reign of Ramesses. Several were with him from the start, including Nebwenenef, named high priest of Amun upon the king's accession, and the vizier Paser, son of Nebneteru, who had been high priest of Amun under Seti I. Ramesses appointed longstanding friends to the highest positions in his administration: the high priest of Amun Bakenkhons; the viceroy Setau; Amenemipet, the loyal "royal messenger to all foreign lands"; and (Ramesses-) Ashahebsed, the official charged with supervising construction of the temples at Abu Simbel. Linked to the royal family by blood or marriage, all of these great men lived in a princely fashion and wove close relationships and networks of supporters among themselves, creating dynasties of senior functionaries and the priesthood. At Abydos, for example, six successive generations of the same family served Osiris. This structure effectively strengthened the new dynasty, though in the long run it fostered internal disputes and injustices.

The role of the vizier

Few documents detail the composition of this massive administrative armature or the precise manner in which it functioned. It is necessary to glean information from extant

Left: a relief portrait of Ramesses's son Khaemwaset.

Below: Ramesses II had many portraits made of the beautiful Nefertari, who died at age 50. Her fine silhouette graces all his monuments and her tomb is the most beautiful of all the queens' burials. There are very few portraits of his other wife, Isetnofret.

The tomb of Nefertari

Nefertari, the "great royal wife, mistress of the Two Lands," was probably a child of Theban nobility. She played an important role at the court of Ramesses II, whom she accompanied in the grand official ceremonies of the kingdom. Below left: her tomb in the Valley of the Queens, near Luxor, is a masterpiece of Egyptian painting, richly decorated with mythological scenes. Gods and goddesses are depicted either alone or with the queen, who worships them or presents offerings to them. Excerpts from the *Book of the Dead* fill the upper spaces of the walls. Above left: on the architrave leading to the hall of sarcophagi, the goddess Maat spreads her wings in a protective gesture. Above: the cartouche of Nefertari. Overleaf: details of her tomb paintings.

decrees, circulars, orders, tax rosters, correspondence among functionaries, records of trials, and above all the long narratives, autobiographical inscriptions, and titularies that adorned the tombs of the wealthy and powerful.

An immensely valuable text, *Duties of the Vizier*, was found in the Theban tomb of the vizier Rekhmira of the 18th Dynasty. It presents a fairly complete description of the scope and activities of the vizier, who was administrative manager of the government, though not a political figure such as a prime minister. He also sometimes acted as the pharaoh's spokesperson. The vizier consulted with the director of the treasury and other functionaries, was administrator of cultivated lands, examined official reports and the records of disputes, planned trips to mines and quarries, and supervised great public works. Aspects of the administration of law, police surveillance of the palace, and contacts with messengers also fell within the vizier's jurisdiction.

During the Ramesside period the administration of Egypt itself was highly decentralized. There were two viziers, one in the south, at Thebes, the other in the north, at Piramesse. The administrator of Nubia, called the Royal Son or viceroy of Kush, was of equal rank with these. (Kush was a name for Upper Nubia; Lower Nubia was Wawat.) Below them were provincial governors and local counselors. The country as a whole was divided into 42 provinces, called *sepat* (a later name is *nomes*).

The treasury was the most important department of the state. It controlled the accounts of receipts and expenditures and verified records. The actual income from taxes and tributes, however, was allocated directly, at the local level. Various institutions were funded thus, including the royal residences, harems, and temples.

The administration of Egyptian state religion

The temples of the principal national gods were also important administrative centers. During Ramesses's

B elow: amulets with the name of the bull god Apis and that of the vizier Paser. His tomb contains fragmented passages of the book called *Duties of the Vizier*. It has been possible to reconstitute the text from another version, found in the tomb of Rekhmira, the vizier whom Thutmose III instructed thus: "Look, the vizier is the copper that protects the gold of his master's house; he lowers his eyes neither before high bureaucrats nor before judges, nor does he take merely anyone as a client…And you shall watch over all that falls within the domain of the law, but also within the rights of the people, assuring justice for all. A judge must [live] with his face bared, as water and wind carries back all that he does."

Left: the career of Bakenkhons is inscribed on his statue. He was a priest who rose to be a member of the high clergy and at about age 60 was named high priest of Amun by Ramesses II. He remained at that post for 25 years. Below: the *shabti*, or funerary figurine, of the vizier Paser.

rule, these grew very powerful and wealthy, becoming key participants in the exploitation of natural resources (especially important were agriculture, livestock breeding, mines, and quarries). Their role in the distribution of goods and the control of economic fluctuations also vastly increased. In particular, the high priests of Amun, Re, and Ptah commanded national prestige. This policy did not necessarily weaken the status of older, local divinities, whose prerogatives were maintained under the Ramesside system.

The New Kingdom Decree of Nauri offers a remarkable documentary example of this. It refers to the status of the temples at the great cult center of Osiris at Abydos, in Upper Egypt. Following an Old Kingdom tradition, Seti I exempted the personnel and property of the cult from taxation or administrative supervision. This temple and its domains thus became economically independent. The decree includes a list of those functionaries of the temple who were permitted to contravene a royal decision, from which we may infer an approximate hierarchy of power among them.

According to Nauri's decree, other tasks and privileges of government were also managed locally, both within Egypt and in its vassal states, so that an effective system of hierarchical organization was developed. In Nubia, for example, the inspection of cargo and import and export of regional goods (gold, ivory, ebony, leopard skins, giraffe leather and tails, and aromatic plants) was controlled by the superintendent, scribe, and inspector of the fortresses that stretched across the territory. Boats for Nile travel could be requisitioned by the viceroy of Nubia and by mercenary captains, comptrollers of the royal domain, and royal messengers. The viceroy and his governors and inspectors were responsible for labor administration, including levying of laborers' taxes, appointments, and transfer of workers from one district to another. Members at every rank of the central and provincial bureaucracies were charged with enforcing decrees from the vizier, chief officers, upper courtiers, and judges to the provincial administrators (the viceroy of Nubia, the superintendent of gold, and the governors), to army officers—in particular charioteers—and liaison officers (inspectors and comptrollers of the royal domain, and all the messengers sent to Kush).

Staff officers organized the highly successful military. The Egyptian

"At the far reaches of Egypt and on the territorial borders with Arabia and Ethiopia lies a region that possesses a great number of gold mines."
Diodorus Siculus,
1st century BC

Below: a map of Ramesside gold mines, 20th Dynasty.

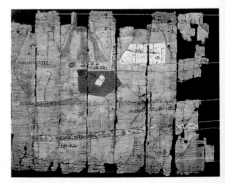

"My master realized that my name was great and beneficent, and then he named me 'Royal Son of Kush'...I brought the taxes of Kush, they being double, and I made certain that the tributes from this country were as plentiful as the sands on the shore—such as was never achieved by any Royal Son of Kush since the time of god [that is, before the earthly kingdom], despite the reach of the powerful arms of the pharaoh, my perfect master."
Stele of Setau, viceroy of Nubia

army filled its ranks through conscription, mercenaries, and career soldiers. Mercenaries played an especially important role in Ramesses's wars.

Under Ramesses II the Asian satellites of Egypt were controlled locally by

Egyptian governors who maintained public order, oversaw the collection of tribute, and represented Egyptian imperial interests. Within limits, they also did their best to impose Egyptian religion, particularly the cult of Amun, "king of the gods." This course was only pursued, however, to the degree possible without supplanting local gods, and Egyptian provincial administrators tended to practice considerable religious tolerance as a matter of prudence. Although each state and city kept its autonomy, its sovereign swore allegiance to the pharaoh, "Sovereign of Sovereigns."

The viceroy of Kush, administrator of Nubia, supervised the land's rich gold mines and collected its tribute. This included exotic produce and rare or precious materials, which were sent by transport boat (above), first to the royal residence, and secondarily to powerful courtiers.

Ramesses II defined himself as the benevolent, nurturing father of Egypt, understanding that the figure of the sovereign embodied *heka,* divinely inspired government. He thus united in his own person religious and administrative rites, and epitomized the well-being and grandeur of the country. Offerings, daily ceremonies, and festivals, as well as the construction and endowment of sacred monuments, represented the health of the empire.

CHAPTER 3
GOVERNMENT AND RITES

Right: the sphinx, a portrait of the pharaoh in animal form, is an image of his sovereignty over nature and men. In this example he grasps a goat-headed vase, which symbolically holds the waters of the Nile. The goat represents Amun, guarantor of abundance through the flood waters. Left: a colossal statue of Ramesses II sits in majesty before the colonnade of his temple at Luxor.

The ritual roles of the pharaoh

The pharaoh's right to rule was granted him by the gods. His earthly government was imbued with *heka* and *maat,* concepts of divine authority and power. Maat was the goddess who personified *maat:* truth, justice, and cosmic harmony. The god Heka, or, more generally, the concept of *heka,* signified the divine creative force that brought the world into being and brought *maat* into the world. The first duty of the pharaoh was therefore to maintain communication with the gods, in order to safeguard victory, prosperity, order, and peace. He performed religious rituals designed to maintain *maat* in Egypt, ensuring that his rule was in accord with the cosmic and social order ordained by the gods. The health of the realm thus depended on the actions of the pharaoh. He made ritual offerings to a statuette of Maat, indicating his ability to carry on the creative work of the gods who had given him life and power, as well as performing rituals and making offerings to other gods. The principal rites were the New Year's ceremonies that confirmed his royal power and jubilees, called *sed* festivals, traditionally held every 30 years. The gods responded to these gifts by granting him the favors that enabled him to bring *maat* to the land. The king, himself the deified son of Re, was the conduit between the people of Egypt and their divinities. As both head of state and religious leader he carried out the work of the gods on earth, maintaining and nourishing the life forces that made Egypt fertile and integrated it into the great cycles of the universe.

The relationships between the

From earliest times, the pharaoh's performance of rituals was the core of his role as leader of the state. Left and above right: an essential rite was the king's offering of Maat to the major divinities, which he alone, as supreme ruler, could carry out. Ritual offerings to the gods by the king gave him a primary and active place in the cycle of life and the rhythms of the cosmos.

pharaoh and the ruling divinities were complex and intricate, expressed in elaborate rites that formed part of the government administration. This rapport between the king and the gods far surpassed simple religious notions of exchange and reciprocity, nor can it be interpreted according to the adage, "God helps those who help themselves."

The pharaoh as the source of all life

Ramesses II learned the lesson perfectly. He made

Ancient Egypt was divided into 42 provinces, or *nomes,* 22 in Upper Egypt and 20 in Lower Egypt. It was incumbent upon the king to perform rites in support of the provinces, which in turn contributed offerings to the national festivals. Left: kneeling figures of men and women personify the provinces whose names are depicted above them. Directly above their heads is the *sepat,* or province symbol: a rectangular plot of land schematically crisscrossed with canals.

innumerable splendid donations to the gods and built countless magnificent monuments and temples, with colossal statues of himself as deified ruler placed prominently in them. He reduced the role of the high priests, setting himself in their place as principal officiant of all the divinities of Egypt. Through this detailed propaganda campaign he established, more than any previous ruler, that the pharaoh was the source of all life.

In this cosmology, the pharaoh shouldered an enormous responsibility, and could not afford to fail in his duties. Among his tasks one of the most important was officiating at the rights of regeneration that celebrated the annual floods of the Nile River. In this way he was linked with the source of Egypt's fertility. The first *sed* festival of Ramesses II, which was celebrated in the thirtieth year of his reign, by chance coincided with a particularly beneficial flooding of the Nile, which filled the valley and flood plain with a bountiful layer of fresh soil. Thereafter jubilees were celebrated at shorter intervals, at first every two to four years, and then almost annually. In Memphis, these festivals were organized by the high priest Khaemwaset until his death; other festivals were celebrated in Piramesse, Upper Egypt, and Nubia at points symbolically

Above: during festivals, oxen were offered to the divinities. These grazing beasts were fattened for sacrifice by trained workers in the temples. The furnishing of an ox for offering was mandated by a royal decree that imposed periodic contributions (one ox per year, for example) on administrators and institutions—a sort of festival tax. The daily diet of most Egyptians comprised cereals, dairy products, eggs, and vegetables, and meat was a luxury reserved for feast days. The meat of sacrificed oxen usually was given to members of the priesthood.

Below: Ramesses II holds the *heka* scepter, whose form mimics an ancient shepherd's crook. It is the symbol of the insignia of the inalienable and absolute sovereignty of the king.

associated with the natural revitalizing phenomenon of the Nile floods.

A beneficent king

Ramesses was thus responsible for the general well-being of the realm. In daily rites the statues of the gods were washed, anointed, perfumed, dressed, and offered food and water. Their meals were then given to the high priests.

In all the 42 provinces of Egypt numerous festivals marked the religious calendar. Cows, sheep, and geese were sacrificed and offerings of the fruits of the harvest were made. Following the ceremonies, these provisions were distributed among the crowds. Workers also received their monthly salaries and food rations at these times. A tacit social contract existed between the pharaoh and his people: through his interactions with the gods, the king would ensure their protection and sustenance; in return the people would give to the sovereign their obedience, homage, and labor.

In this rich and opulent nation, royal generosity benefited not only the great temples and political institutions, but also every stratum of the population, down to the most humble. Under Ramesses's rule, soldiers' salaries were increased and artisans were well paid.

Fostering the gold industry of Nubia

Ramesses also concerned himself with public works of all sorts. Egypt's gold mines lay mainly in Nubia and the eastern desert region and were among its greatest assets, greatly enriching the gods and their temples. Indeed, the oldest known geological map is a diagram of a gold mine from the reign of Ramesses IV (see page 54). The health of the miners and metalworkers of Nubia was therefore guarded with care. Under Seti I, an attempt had been made to establish a good water supply for them: a temple had been constructed and wells dug in the gold mines at Wadi Mia, and in an inscription at Quban, Ramesses recalled that at the Nubian gold deposits of Wadi Allaqi his father had directed water drilling (unfortunately fruitless) to proceed to a depth of 20 cubits (approximately 200 feet, or 60 meters). Ramesses wished to

Above: a pectoral ornament worn by Ramesses II. Goldsmiths worked under the patronage of the god Ptah at Memphis, and the metal held religious and symbolic connotations: "Gold is the flesh of the gods; it does not belong to you. Also take care not to say what Re said at the beginning of language: 'My skin is made of gold, fine and pure!' As to Amun, the lord of my temple, his two eyes are on his possessions. And they do not want to be stripped of their goods."
Seti I's Decree of Kanais to the gold panners of Wadi Mia

The flood waters of the Nile were associated, in religious terms, with the primordial fluid from which all life emerged. The periodic floods brought abundance and nourishment to an otherwise arid and desert land. Left: a scene of two Nile gods, or water spirits, carrying seeds of fertility. Fish, birds, and aquatic vegetation surround them, emphasizing the life-giving powers of water.

surpass his father's project, himself commissioning new wells. The stele at Quban notes that since the viceroy of Nubia continued to lament the lack of water for his workers, Ramesses appealed to the gods (in particular to Hapy, the divinity of the Nile floods), whereupon water miraculously began to gush at a depth of 12 cubits—little more than 20 feet (6 meters).

Below: a goldsmith at work, in a mural painting in the tomb of Rekhmira in the Theban Valley of the Nobles.

Architectural patronage

An important obligation of the pharaoh was to authorize religious artworks. These included the making and ornamentation of statues of the gods, the building of luxurious temples to house them, the enrichment of their treasuries, and the consecration of gigantic obelisks. Small statues were made of gold and silver, representing the gods' flesh and bones; colossal figures were sculpted in painted stone.

The horse was introduced into Egypt with great success in the 17th century BC. Ramesses II, like Thutmose III and Amenhotep II before him, loved his horses. His favorites, named Victory in Thebes and Mut Is Pleased, pulled his chariot at the battle of Qadesh, and he immortalized them on a gold ring, left.

Ramesses II left his mark throughout Upper and Lower Egypt, both by commissioning his own works and by usurping those of his predecessors. In some cases his intention was not to obscure the achievements of past sovereigns, but to exalt his ancestors. From Palestine to Nubia, ruined temples, many dedicated to Amun, carry his name, and many are the stelae that he erected throughout the empire. At Abydos, he completed the construction work begun by his father, Seti I, and then erected his own temple there, displaying a list of royal ancestors that excluded the kings who ruled during times of crisis (called the intermediate periods), as well as those of the Amarna interval.

The biblical Exodus of the Jews from Egypt is generally thought to date from the reign of Ramesses II, though no such episode appears in Egyptian records, or to be linked to the expulsion of the Hyksos by Ahmose. However, it is often speculated that Jewish captives worked on the construction of Piramesse. Below: a fanciful evocation of the story.

He added to the embellishment of the temple of Set (patron of the pharaoh and his lineage) at Avaris, near Piramesse. In Memphis, Heliopolis, and Thebes, Ramesses II expanded the great existing temples. Starting in the early years of his reign, he developed the religious precinct at Karnak, completing its great hypostyle hall and enlarging the nearby temple at Luxor with an antecourt and pylon (a massive ceremonial gateway), accented with monumental statues and two obelisks.

On the west bank of the Nile at Thebes, he consecrated a statue to the goddess Hathor in the village of the workmen who constructed the royal tombs, now called Deir el-Medina. Most magnificent of all were

The name Moses is rendered in Egyptian as Mes, which means "the Child" (of a god). Many foreign children were raised in the royal court, and it is possible that a Hebrew noble's son might have been among them.

Ramesses II contributed a good deal of new architecture to the religious and political capital of Thebes, on the west bank of the Nile, and Luxor, directly across the river. Above: the Ramesseum was both a political and a theological center, and was famous for its vineyards as well. He expanded the Temple of Amun at Luxor. This institution was in the forefront of religious, economic, and cultural activities, not only during his reign, but under his successors. In his second year as king he constructed a pylon (below, far left) at its entrance, preceded by colossal statues of him and two obelisks, one of which was given to France by the pasha Mohammed Ali in 1836, and is now in the Place de la Concorde, Paris. Ramesses probably usurped these from previous rulers, since the hieroglyphics on the median line of each face appear to have been recut, and the lateral lines to have been newly engraved. Near left: another view of the Temple of Amun.

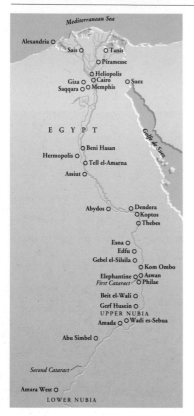

the funerary temple he built for himself, intended to endure for "a million years," the Ramesseum, and the so-called Tomb of Ozymandias, whose romantic ruins have set so many poets and artists to dreaming.

The great provincial centers were not forgotten. In Middle Egypt, for example, Ramesses II endowed the temple of Hermopolis with a new sanctuary that was further decorated by his successors Merenptah and Seti II. Hermopolis was sacred to the eight primordial gods, plus Thoth, god of wisdom and master of places.

But it was in Nubia that Ramesses constructed the greatest number of temples: seven sanctuaries in six different sites along the length of the Nile, following the line of the royal gold mines. The oldest, at Beit el-Wali, south of Aswan, was founded at the beginning of his reign and decorated during its first two years; the series continued to Amara West, near the Third Cataract of the Nile.

Abu Simbel

The general fame of the Nubian temples of Ramesses II was eclipsed by one in

Left: principal sites of the Nile Valley. Below: statues of ensign-bearers such as this one became common under Ramesses II. The ensign, a sacred staff crowned by an aegis, symbolized the deity associated with the royal *ka*, the immortal and divine spirit of the king. Right: Queen Nefertari affectionately places a hand on the calf of the colossus of Ramesses II.

particular: Abu Simbel. This formidable complex of buildings lies approximately 41 miles (70 kilometers) north of the Second Cataract of the Nile. It is a double *speos,* or rock temple, cut into the side of a cliff that faces the river. Buried in deep sand until its rediscovery in the 19th century AD, saved from the flooding caused by the construction of the Aswan Dam in the 20th, it stands today as an enduring record of its patron's greatness.

The site had long been sacred. Two hills, the Meha and the Ibshek, stand some 500 feet (150 meters) apart, overlooking the Nile (now Lake Nasser, above the modern dam). There Ramesses II chose to pay homage to his tutelary gods, entrusting to their care the annual beneficent flood of the Nile, and glorifying the principal events of his reign and life. The great temple at Abu Simbel, carved into the mountain at Meha, is dedicated to Ramesses II, as well as to the three great gods—Amun, Re, and Ptah. To the north of it, a small rock-hewn temple was cut into the mountain of Ibshek, sacred to the goddess Hathor, the primordial mother, patroness of love, music, and joy. This was consecrated jointly to the goddess and to Ramesses's wife Nefertari.

The double temple was completed in approximately year 21 of Ramesses's reign (though the wall decorations were finished some 13 years later). In front of the trapezoidal entry of the great temple are four 65-foot (20-meter) colossal seated statues of the pharaoh (one of them has deteriorated badly). These are flanked by much smaller representations of members of his family, including Nefertari and several of the royal children. The first hall contains eight ornamented pillars, 33 feet (10 meters) in height, that bear representations of the god Osiris, whose features are those of Ramesses.

On the walls of this first hall and of a subsequent vestibule with square pillars that leads into the sanctuary is a series of images depicting the two functions of the king: *sekhem* is represented by ritual scenes of the massacre of enemies, the epic unfolding of the great battle at Qadesh; *heka* government is illustrated by images of cult ceremonies and scenes of offerings presented to the divinities by Ramesses. At the far end of

When the Nile was dammed above the First Cataract at Aswan in 1971, the site of Abu Simbel was inundated by the artificially created Lake Nasser. The temples were moved to higher ground, near their original position. Above: a detail of the great seated figures before the main temple.

Ramesses II assigned management of construction of Abu Simbel to a man of Asian origins, who seems to have held the title of royal wine bearer. His name was Egyptianized as "Many Would Be the Jubilees [of Ramesses]." Overleaf, page 72: exterior views of the two temples, cut directly into the stone cliffs; the great temple is at left, the small temple at right. At the entrance of the latter stand statues of Ramesses II, Queen Nefertari, and their children. In images within the temple the queen, represented as a personification of the star Sirius (a reference to the goddess Sopdet, or Sothis), is greeted by Hathor, the mother-goddess and deity of beginnings.

The two temples were set at angles to one another and to the Nile, so that their axes intersected in the middle of its course. The scholar Christiane Desroches Noblecourt proposes an interpretation of the temples that links their orientation, the gods to whom they were dedicated, and the astronomical conjunction, every 70 days, of the sun and the star Sirius—which, in July, would occur at the same time as the long-awaited arrival of the Nile flood. Page 73: the inner sanctuary of the great temple.

the sanctuary, deep within the hill, four colossal rock-hewn statues represent the proprietary gods of the site: Re-Harakhte, the deified Ramesses II, Amun-Re, and Ptah. On the temple's facade, above the entrance door, is an image portraying an offering by Ramesses of the goddess Maat to Re-Harakhte. It takes the form of a rebus comprising the words *user, maat,* and *re,* elements of the name Ramesses, and signals the highly symbolic nature of the temple, whose magnificent presence proclaims the power of the pharaoh.

"His Majesty has built a fortified residence. 'Great Are His Victories' is its name. It stretches between Phoenicia and the beloved country [Egypt] and is filled with food and nourishments...The palace of the city is similar to the two horizons of the sky and 'Ramesses, Beloved of Amun' is there as its god; 'Montu in the Two Lands' is its herald; 'Sun of Princes' is its vizier; 'Joy of Egypt, Beloved of Amun' is its nomarch."

Hymn to Piramesse

Civic architecture

Ramesses carried out his dreams of grandeur in the construction of Piramesse, a dazzlingly beautiful capital, decorated in the auspicious color, turquoise blue. There he built his Residence, the seat of government. All the central bureaucracies were housed there, under the direction of the vizier of the north, who worked in close collaboration with the sovereign.

In addition to the administrative center at Piramesse, there were three other religious and political capitals: Memphis, sacred to the god Ptah; Heliopolis, belonging to the god Re; and Thebes, city of Amun, King of the Gods, where the vizier of the south resided. Of course

Below: the ruins of Tanis in the eastern Delta, which Ramesses built using materials from Avaris, which he destroyed.

these too received the attentions of Ramesses II, as did his harem at Mi-Wer, in the Fayum region, just south of the Delta point.

Divine statues

Ramesses II erected statues of himself throughout the empire, a practice that had been popularized by Amenhotep III's Colossi of Memnon. Many of these sculptural portraits were in monumental scale, and they usually presented the pharaoh in his deified guise. Most bore evocative epithets: "Re of the Sovereigns," "Sovereign of Sovereigns," "Montu [the god of war] in the Two Lands," "Living Image of Ramesses in the Land of the Ark" (i.e., Nubia). Like the cult statues of the other gods, these figures were maintained by priests, paid by endowment. In this way, Ramesses multiplied his divine presence across the vast territory of his empire, physically manifesting his power from Upper Nubia in the south to Syria in the north.

The Ramesses II style

Monumental art—and in particular sacred art—was intended to

The royal city of Piramesse, in the eastern Delta, was built near modern-day Qantir. Left: a lacquered and engraved brick from the site. Above: an enameled plaque from Qantir.

A vanished capital

"I arrived at the House of Ramesses, Beloved of Amun [Pi-Ramesses], and I found it extremely prosperous. It is a very beautiful place that, although it resembles Thebes, has no equal. It was Re himself who was its founder. Life in the Residence is pleasant; its fields abound with all sorts of good produce; each day it is well endowed with food. Its canals are filled with fish, and its marsh-lands with birds; its prairies are abundant with green pastures;...from the cultivated fields come fruit with the taste of honey. Its granaries are filled with barley and wheat...Every day in the city there is a great abundance of food; and everyone who resides there is delighted, they have not even a desire to speak. There, the common people are as the great people. Come, so that we may celebrate its festivals of the sky and of the start of the seasons... The young people of the city "Great Are Its Victories" [name of Pi-Ramesses] each day dress [for the festival]; sweet olive oil is spread on their heads, and their hair is again styled."

Letter written by the scribe Pabasa to his superior, the scribe Amenemopet

L eft: a modern recon-struction of Piramesse.

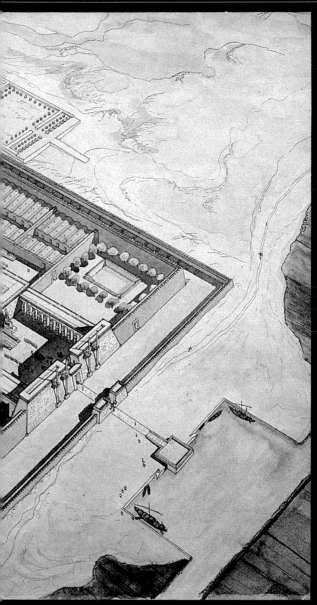

The Ramesseum

At Thebes, just north of the Colossi of Memnon, stood the funerary temple of Ramesses II, the so-called Temple of a Million Years, today known as the Ramesseum (left: a modern reconstruction). It was a precinct surrounded by a wall of unbaked brick, within which were the temple, built of stone; a palace to the north of it; a small temple, dedicated to Seti I and his wife Tuyu, in the southeast corner; and numerous other buildings. Many of these were constructed of bricks stamped with the name of Ramesses. On the north, west, and south sides, avenues of sphinxes surrounded the wall. The site is entered at the east. Following the east–west axis, one passes through two successive pylons and crosses two peristyle courts lined with Osiride pillars. These lead to the hypostyle hall, whose vault was supported by 48 campaniform columns in the central nave. Three progressively smaller and darker rooms then lead to the sanctuary, in which lies the barque of Amun, used during festival processions. In the courts, colossal statues of Ramesses frame the gates; the damaged colossus called Ramesses, Sun of the Sovereigns originally measured more than 55 feet (17 meters) tall.

make manifest the grandeur of the empire and to celebrate its inhabitants, both divine and human. The art style that flourished in the reign of Ramesses II was notably grand and imposing. The two most significant examples of it are the rock-hewn temples at Abu Simbel, and the Ramesseum at Luxor, on the west bank of the Nile at Thebes.

The basic floor plan of an Egyptian Middle Kingdom temple was definitively established under Ramesses II. A massive pylon and a trapezoidal entry lead to one or more courts, which give onto a hypostyle hall with three naves (a high central nave and two lower side naves), formed by giant columns. Beyond this space lies a series of progressively narrower and darker halls and chapels, which culminate in the sanctuary in whose shadows resides the tabernacle of the god.

These sites were decorated with colossal statues, obelisks, wall paintings, and reliefs rich in color and detail. The artists of Ramesses's temples broke with the old Egyptian decorative tradition in which scenes appear in horizontal bands, called registers. They adapted elements of the radical Amarna style, and

filled all available wall and column surfaces with scenes of ceremonies and battles. These artworks—notably several episodes depicting the battle at Qadesh at Abu Simbel—show great movement, energy, and dramatic intensity.

The Ramesses II style also used high relief, as opposed to the more traditional bas-relief; this technique dates from the second year of the pharaoh's reign. This innovation enhanced the effects of light and shadow on the carved images, and draws the viewer's attention to the presence of the sun. Ramesses was always mindful of sun symbolism, and gave it universal and imperial dimensions. Indeed, he attached a second element to his name: Setepenre, or the Chosen of Re.

"O chosen and valiant workers, I know your hand, which carves for me my many monuments. Oh you who cherish working with precious stones of every kind, who cut into the granite and fit together the quartzite, brave and powerful [men]: since you have constructed the monuments, thanks to you I shall be able to adorn all the temples I have erected for the length of their existence…I am Ramesses, Beloved of Amun, he who enables the younger generation to grow by giving them life… I shall provide for all of your needs; and thus you shall work for me with a heart filled with love."

Stele of the 8th year, from Manshiyet es-Sadr (Heliopolis)

Left: the Temple of Amun at Luxor; below: a fragment from the Ramesseum.

To protect Egypt from its enemies was one of the prime duties of the sovereign, who not only suppressed revolts and repelled invaders, but sought ever to extend his country's borders. He was able to accomplish these things by grace of the divine power called *sekhem.*

CHAPTER 4
POWER AND DOMINION

Left: the image of bound captives, a clear symbol of triumph, appears frequently in pharaonic reliefs and wall paintings, such as this detail from Abu Simbel. Right: Ramesses II wore this heavy bracelet of gold and lapis lazuli. Splendid golden finery, jewels, and precious objects were a mark of the prestige and power of the pharaoh.

The king's twofold divine power

Sekhem comprised those royal acts, often violent, designed to maintain, impose, or restore *maat* in the land and drive away its antithesis, *isfet*.

On the verso of the ancient Narmer Palette (page 31) is a scene depicting the king massacring enemies, an emblematic representation of *sekhem*. On this document, violent acts (*sekhem*) were associated with the White Crown; the recto (page 30) bears scenes of ritual acts (*heka*), associated with the Red Crown. Somewhat later in the reign of Narmer the two crowns came to signify Upper and Lower Egypt, respectively. Soon thereafter, the crowns were combined to form the Double Crown, signifying a single power. This concept came to be known as the Two Powers, or *pa sekhemty,* an expression the ancient Greeks later transformed into *pschent,* the headdress of double magical power worn by the pharaohs.

The annual flooding of the Nile was the source of Egypt's astonishing fertility in the heart of the desert. The wealth of the land was therefore essentially agricultural, and the farming cycle was dictated by a calendar of three seasons: floods, planting, and harvest. Each season comprised 4 months of 30 days each, to which 5 days were added at the end of the year to keep the cycle consonant with that of the moon. Left: a scene of harvesting wheat with a sickle, from a tomb painting.

Master of war and agriculture

On the great Macehead of King Scorpion (page 28), the king, dressed in a richly decorated short loincloth and wearing the White Crown, holds a hoe and prepares to cleave the earth, actively and violently, in order to sow seed. (The Narmer Macehead bears corresponding scenes of ritual relating to animal husbandry.) The symbolic act of *sekhem* shown on this early ceremonial object served as a reference for all subsequent pharaohs: the sovereign drove off chaos and disorder and fertilized (that is, made active) fallow land. He was absolute master of the sun; under the sun, he was sole owner of the Egyptian earth, which was bequeathed to him by Horus, son and legitimate heir of Osiris, divine forerunner of the earthly kings.

The pharaoh, in turn, entrusted the care and exploitation of the land to the administration of the temples, and to his close relatives. But he himself remained the ultimate proprietor.

Through records of ceremonies in documents and artworks, it is possible to trace the traditions that link the White Crown and *sekhem* with the defense of the country and agricultural management; both were directly dependent upon the king's personal power and royal charisma.

B elow: the pharaoh wears the *khepresh,* the Blue Crown, representing the kingdom in all its aspects. Opposite: the god Horus wears the *pschent,* the Double Crown representing sovereign power.

First military campaigns

While the first years of the reign of Ramesses II were largely devoted to a vast program of construction, the young sovereign took up arms on two

occasions. In year 2 of his reign, he was obliged to
drive back an assault by a people called the Sea People,
apparently pirates of Shardana origins (Philistine, or
Palestinian), who had settled on the Delta islands.
Defeated in naval combat, the Shardana were drafted
into the pharaoh's armies, where they proved to be
quite brave and were repaid with land allotments.
In year 4, Benteshina, vassal king of Amurru, a
territory in Syria, shifted his allegiance from the
Hittite Empire (in what is now Anatolia, in Turkey)
to Egyptian overlordship. The Hittites contested this,
and in response Ramesses brought an army north,
securing the area around what is now Lebanon and

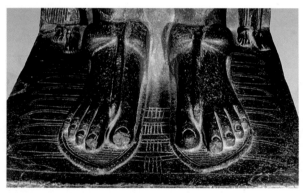

Syria with Egyptian garrisons in Canaan, Tyre, and
Byblos. He then returned to Egypt by way of
Phoenicia.

But the following year the Hittite king Muwatallis
challenged Ramesses once more, and the quarrel
between the two empires culminated in a great battle
near the Orontes River, around the fortified town of
Qadesh, in Syria.

Royal courage

The epic battle of Qadesh is depicted on the walls of
the great temples at Abydos, Karnak, Abu Simbel, and
the Ramesseum, accompanied by inscriptions, as well

Following its first appearance on the Palette of Narmer, the ritual scene of the pharaoh massacring the enemy or subjugating prisoners was frequently depicted. Ramesses II is usually shown this way, manifesting his universal and imperial power. Far left: the feet of the pharaoh symbolically trample the Nine Bows, representing the conquest of foreign enemies. "The chiefs of all the foreign lands are beneath your sandals," declares the inscription on the obelisk of Ramesses II now in Paris. Near left: on a stele, Ramesses is shown grasping three prisoners by the hair, so that they are both physically and symbolically in his hands. The three represent the three primary ethnic groups that surrounded Egypt—Africans, Asians, and Libyans—over whom, in principle, the pharaoh held dominion. The power of the king over his adversaries was expressed in a variety of ways: in works of art, in laws, and through magical practices such as the ritual destruction of statuettes representing enemies, accompanied by incantations.

as recounted in two Egyptian manuscript narratives, a report referred to as
the *Bulletin,* and a longer, more literary
and lyrical text called the *Poem.* These
tell the story as one of the king's
personal heroism.

The true outcome of the battle
was indecisive—neither victory nor
defeat—but this mattered less to
Egypt's official historians than the feat
of arms claimed by Ramesses himself.
On his chariot, either alone or
accompanied only by his personal
guard, the pharaoh confronted the
ranks of the Hittite army. He is so
depicted in numerous paintings and
documents: supremely brave, the true son of his
father, Amun, the chosen, the beloved of Re and
Amun, the god-king upon whom his people could
depend.

A bove: a fragment of
the papyrus manu-
script of a long, lyrical
epic poem titled *The
Battle of Qadesh.*

The battle of Qadesh

The tale as recorded in Egypt is this: in year 5 of his
reign (c. 1274 BC), on the ninth day of the second month
of summer, the pharaoh left Piramesse and traveled with
a great military force toward Canaan, in Palestine, to
meet and defeat the
Hittites, who were
moving south to
give battle. He took
four army divisions,
named for the four
tutelary gods,
Amun, Re, Ptah,
and Set. He
approached
Qadesh, the
Hittites' southern
defensive fort, by
a coastal route,
rather than
crossing the

plains of Bekaa (in Lebanon). The *Bulletin* recounts that after a stop in "the mountainous region to the south of Qadesh," the king moved north, toward a ford of the Orontes River.

On the way, he met two Shosu (Bedouins), members of tribes subject to the Hittites; these swore allegiance to him and reported that the Hittite army was still far to the north, near Aleppo. They were, however, spies sent by Muwatallis to mislead the Egyptians. The pharaoh fell for the ploy, crossed the Orontes with the Amun division, and took up a position to the northwest of Qadesh. The Re division was still fording the river, and the Ptah and Set divisions were in the distant south, when two captured Hittite spies, having been beaten, revealed that the Hittite army was actually very close, hiding behind the fortified city and ready to engage.

Messengers were dispatched to the rear to hurry the Ptah division forward. The Amun division, busy setting up camp, was caught off guard, and a unit of

In the army of Ramesses II, the bow was the preferred weapon of chariot soldiers. Below: daggers and a curved, double-edged sword, called a *khepesh* (inspired by the Asian *harpe*, or scimitar) were standard equipment for foot soldiers, who also carried lances and javelins.

Ramesses II commissioned scenes from the battle of Qadesh to decorate monuments throughout the empire. Left: a reconstruction drawing of the facade of the pylon at the temple of Luxor. The convention of Egyptian wall decoration was to present a sequence of scenes in clearly demarcated horizontal bands, or registers. Ramesses's pylon departs from this approach to depict the battle in a single, vast pictorial field that offers a greater sense of realism.

The battle of Qadesh

The Egyptian chariot was a weapon of war, light, fast, and maneuverable. It was drawn by a pair of horses and occupied by two people, the driver and the warrior. The title of Driver of His Majesty's Chariot was a prestigious one. Enviable too were the professions of royal horse breeder and manager of the royal stud farms, which were reserved for members of the nobility. Here and overleaf: sections of bas-relief, and reconstruction drawings of them, from Ramesses's temple at Abu Simbel depict the military feats of the king and his royal triumph. Above center: he subdues his enemies while Amun presents him the *khepesh* of victory.

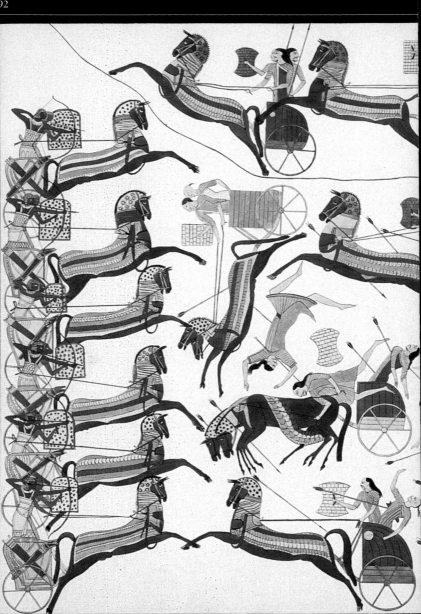

Hittite charioteers suddenly appeared and scattered the Re division at the river crossing. At this critical moment, Ramesses, arrayed in battle dress, mounted his own chariot, hitched with his favorite horses, and launched into battle, roaring his battle cry. He fought like the god Montu himself, spreading panic among the enemy. Just then the Nearin, an Egyptian detachment stationed in Amurru, came out to the aid of the pharaoh, probably with the assistance of Egyptian elements who had regrouped, and the Hittite onslaught was halted. The Egyptian camp was apparently not overrun, for the children of Ramesses found relative safety there.

The following morning, the experienced Egyptian army rallied and prepared to launch an assault, whereupon the Hittite king called for an armistice. The pharaoh consulted his military staff and accepted this offer,

Egypt remained at odds with the Hittite empire until the signing of the Egyptian–Hittite treaty. Numerous bas-reliefs in the Ramesseum, Luxor, and elsewhere record the strife. Above: officers of Ramesses II at the battle of Qadesh, in a bas-relief in the Ramesseum; above right: Hittite soldiers flee before the Egyptian army, in a scene at Abu Simbel. Left: the king of the Hittites, Muwatallis, died about year 10 of Ramesses's reign, creating a crisis of succession. His son, Urhi-Teshub, whose mother was a concubine, fought with his paternal uncle for the throne. It was the latter, Hattusilis III, worried about Assyrian expansionism, who concluded the treaty in year 21. Opposite: two seals of the Hittite kings.

Before the battle of Qadesh, Ramesses addressed an emotional prayer to Amun: "I call upon you, oh my father, Amun. I am amidst innumerable enemies whom I do not know; all the alien countries are united against me, and I am utterly alone...But I realize that Amun values me more than

and the Egyptian army returned home without further incident. As soon as Ramesses had withdrawn, however, Muwatallis evicted Benteshina and retook Amurru.

The Egyptian–Hittite rivalry

Egypt and the Hittite Empire remained in conflict for another 15 years, contesting control of the states and cities that lay between them. These were constantly changing alliances, either by conquest or as suited their own interests. The chief bones of contention were Amurru and the province of Upi, near Damascus. In years 8 and 9, Ramesses's armies advanced as far as Deper, and reached Tunip. Each of the two empires, however, also had a second front to worry about: Assyria threatened the Hittites, while the Egyptians had to defend themselves against the Libyans to the west.

In addition, a dynastic crisis had weakened the Hittites. Upon the death of Muwatallis, two pretenders disputed the throne. One was Urhi-Teshub, who reigned under the name of Mursilis III and was illegitimate. The other was his uncle, the legitimate heir, Hattusilis III,

the millions of soldiers, more than a few hundred thousand chariots, more than ten thousand men, brothers and children joined with a single heart...He [Amun] cried out: 'Face to face with you, Ramesses, Beloved of Amun! I am with you. It is I, your father. My hand is in your own. I count for more than the hundreds of thousands of men, I the master of victory, who love bravery.' "

who ultimately prevailed in his right to the throne. Exiled to the farthest reaches of the empire, Uhri-Teshub took refuge in Egypt during year 18 of the reign of Ramesses II. Hattusilis III demanded the extradition of his nephew, but Ramesses refused, and war once more threatened. The armies of Egypt were readied for battle, but as Assyrian power meanwhile brought pressure to bear on the Hittite borders, Hattusilis III was forced to negotiate a peace with Ramesses.

The first great international treaty

The outcome of these peace talks was a treaty written on a silver tablet in the official international language, Akkadian, and signed by Ramesses II and Hattusilis III in year 21 of the former's reign. Copies on clay tablets were kept at Hattusas, the Hittite capital. Egyptian translations, written on papyrus, were placed in the records office in Piramesse, and a version was inscribed on an immense wall stele at Karnak. The accord called for the permanent cessation of hostilities between the two powers, as well as mutual concessions: Egypt withdrew from Amurru, but kept the province of Upi and confirmed its rights over Phoenician shipping ports. Emissaries of the pharaoh were declared free to travel the length of the international trade routes, as far as Ugarit.

This treaty contained some astonishingly modern clauses: the promise of peace and fraternity; a pact declaring nonaggression and mutual assistance; laws safeguarding the

Peace and brotherhood were the catchwords of the treaty concluded between Ramesses II and Hattusilis III and guaranteed by all the Egyptian and Hittite gods. Above: a frieze of 12 Hittite gods at the sanctuary of Yazilikaya, in Anatolia. On the front face of the silver tablet on which the treaty was inscribed is a representation of the god Sutekh embracing an image of the high chief of Hatti, surrounded by the words: "The guarantee of Sutekh, king of the sky, is the guarantee of the treaty made by Hattusilis, high chief of Hatti, the strong, son of Mursil, the high chief of Hatti, the strong."

rights of the monarchy in both states and warranting the extradition of fugitives; and amnesty for refugees. The thousand gods and goddesses of Hatti and the thousand gods and goddesses of Egypt played the role, so to speak, of an international coalition guaranteeing the treaty, promising retribution against whomever broke it, and blessings on all those who respected it.

The pharaoh thus magnificently fulfilled his fundamental obligations as son and heir to the gods. An era of peace and prosperity, even of opulence, followed the war, and Egypt experienced decades of well-being, until the death of Ramesses II.

The marriage of Ramesses II to the daughter of Hattusilis III

From the time of the treaty, good relations existed between the two lands, with the kings writing to one another and the great royal wives, Nefertari and Pudukhepa, queen of Hatti, exchanging greetings and news. Friendly visits were made by both parties, while the memory of old disagreements (such as the sheltering of Urhi-Teshub at the court of Piramesse) dimmed with the passage of time. The two sovereigns decided to seal this increasingly stable alliance with a marriage. Hattusilis offered the hand of his eldest daughter to Ramesses, embellishing the gift with a fine dowry of servants, cattle, and horses.

When he accepted this offer with zeal, Ramesses certainly must have had in his mind's eye the image of Amenhotep III welcoming his Mitannian wife, Gilukhepa, accompanied by many courtiers and all the treasures of the East. Representatives promptly entered into lively negotiations and eventually a bridal procession was formed, under the watchful eyes of the

The marriage of Ramesses II to the eldest daughter of Hattusilis III cemented the alliance. A marriage stele at Abu Simbel records: "When the daughter of the king of Hatti arrived in Egypt, soldiers, charioteers and dignitaries of His Majesty escorted her, mixing with the soldiers and charioteers of Hatti, forming a single army composed of Asian and Egyptian soldiers; they

ate and drank together, and like brothers they shared a single heart; no one rejected another, peace and brotherhood dwelt among them, according to the designs of god himself, the king of Upper and Lower Egypt, Usermaatre Setepenre, son of Re, Ramesses Beloved of Amun, blessed with life." Above: a redrawn detail of the stele; left: fragment of a letter from Ramesses II to Hattusilis III, concerning the marriage.

Hittite gods. An Egyptian escort left to meet the Hittite princess, who arrived with the promised dowry and lavish gifts. She was anointed with Egyptian oils and given the Egyptian name Manefrure. At court she lived in the company of the other royal wives—Isetnofret, Nefertari, and their daughters, the princess-wives— before moving to the harem at Mi-Wer, in the Fayum region. In about year 40 of his reign, Ramesses II married a second daughter of Hattusilis, who was also furnished with a rich dowry; the new marriage was less sensational, however.

The king as justice of the peace

The use of military and police force to preserve domestic tranquillity and economic prosperity, two aspects of *maat,* was governed by the *sekhem* of the pharaoh.

Whenever necessary, the king himself intervened personally to maintain public order. We have a remarkably detailed description of such an event, recorded in a rather literary fashion on an ostracon (a limestone fragment). In about year 30 of the reign of Ramesses II, at the time of his first jubilee, the unscrupulous director of several temple storehouses or granaries at Thebes was skimming for himself a portion

The Ramesseum, the mortuary temple of Ramesses II, played an important role in the economic life of the country, as the ruins of its vast vaulted store-houses (below) still attest.

Goods used at the temple—as offerings and as food for the priests and staff—were stored there, as was the plentiful produce of the complex's land holdings. The Ramesseum possessed a center of financial services, a library, and a scribal school; among its other responsibilities, it provided for the artisans in the nearby village of Deir el-Medina who built and decorated the tombs in the Valley of the Kings.

of the goods donated to the gods and the cults of past kings, and hiding them at his father's house. These thefts were not minor. Thanks to the man's careful book-keeping, a list of the stolen items can be drawn up: several hundred pieces of linen clothing and pairs of leather sandals; an enormous quantity of copper ingots, tools, and pots and pans; 3 fully equipped chariots; livestock (30 bulls, 10 goats, 30 geese); 5 jugs of wine; and 20,000 sacks of grain. When he was named inspector of herds of the pastures in an area in the Delta region called the Borders, this fellow left his wife and daughter in Thebes to continue his trafficking. A simple scribe named Hatyay noticed the style of their household and

filed a complaint against the women for visiting the storehouses without the knowledge of the comptrollers.

Upon interrogation, the wife explained that since her husband had been the administrator of the warehouses she had leave to enter them. The husband was then summoned and defended himself, swearing that the merchandise he had spirited away had already been taken back by the police, and that these same officers had also treated him badly the previous year, and that he was going to submit a complaint against them. He would, he declared, address the pharaoh himself during the jubilee!

Wine, a luxury product, was intended for the royal residence and the tables of the upper nobility. Above: scribes labeling the jars of a new vintage, in a tomb painting. The Ramesseum seems to have had its own vineyards, and also to have been the administrative seat of several wine-producing regions.

The case came to court and Ramesses II assigned his son, the heir, to judge it. Unfortunately, the conclusion is unknown, as the ostracon ends there.

Agricultural management and land division

Ramesses II proved himself an able domestic as well as military administrator, attentive to the

management, distribution, and improvement of agricultural lands—essential to both prosperity and popular contentment. Had we no documents concerning his land policies, they could be deduced from a

Right: the sacred geese of Amun, from Deir el-Medina.

comparison of texts of prior and subsequent reigns, which reveal his many reforms.

Under this pharaoh, Egypt grew rich beyond imagining. A correspondence between the chief of the treasury, Panehsy, and a priest of Amun named Hori, dating to year 24 of his reign, attests to the remarkable level of wealth achieved during his regime, and numerous inscriptions confirm that he endowed his statues as if they were the gods themselves.

The Greek historian Herodotus, writing in the 5th century BC, reports that Ramesses (whom he calls Sesostris) distributed land in equal, square lots, creating tenures for loyal officers and soldiers (see page 146). The 1st-century BC historian Diodorus Siculus repeats Herodotus's account:

"In command of the several divisions of his troops he set his companions, who were by this time inured to warfare, had striven after a reputation for valor from their youth, and cherished with a brotherly love both their king and one another, the number of them being over seventeen hundred. And upon all these commanders he bestowed allotments of the best land in Egypt, in order that, enjoying sufficient income and lacking nothing, they might sedulously practise the art of war."

Above left: a procession of dignitaries, from Thebes.

Agriculture in ancient Egypt was managed by the temples. In the New Kingdom, these grew very wealthy and acted as powerful intermediaries between the central government and local farmers. Ramesses II carried out an important program of land redistribution, recorded by both Herodotus and the Papyrus Wilbour, a fiscal document from the reign of Ramesses V. An immense text known as the Great Harris Papyrus, the longest surviving ancient Egyptian document (135 feet, or 41 meters), records an extraordinary donation of land by Ramesses III (74,000 acres, or 30,000 hectares) to the temples. This gift was probably a continuation of the agrarian policies of Ramesses II.

From the time of the Old Kingdom, Egyptian scribes maintained careful and detailed fiscal records, using an accurate system of accounting and standardized weights and measures. This was essential to an efficient bureaucracy and a healthy economy. Opposite: a scribe from the estate of Amun Neferrenpet oversees the weighing and recording of the harvest.

The long reign of Ramesses II, opulent and sumptuous, witnessed increasing wealth throughout Egypt. With prosperity came improved social conditions and a cultural flowering. Artisans, jurists, architects, doctors, scribes, and artists all contributed to making the era of Ramesses II brilliant and eternally memorable.

CHAPTER 5
TO LIVE AND ENDURE

The artisans of Deir el-Medina made handsome, decorated private tombs for themselves as well as those of the kings and nobles. Left: in a wall painting in his tomb, the worker Pashedu quenches his thirst under a palm tree. The colors of his funerary vault remain astonishingly fresh. Right: a wooden case for a scale from the tomb of the architect Kha and his wife Merit.

The workmen's village at Deir el-Medina

Much of the greatest art of pharaonic Egypt is to be found in its tombs. The cult and traditions relating to the afterlife required kings and nobles to construct lavish burial rooms for themselves, many of which have survived through the centuries because they were hidden underground, in the arid earth of the desert.

The ancient village of Deir el-Medina lay on the west bank of the Nile, opposite Luxor, under the sacred mountain that overlooks the Valleys of the Kings and Queens, home to some 150 magnificent royal tombs. In this small village, from the beginning of the 18th Dynasty through the end of the 20th (almost half a millennium), lived the generations of workers and artists who excavated, constructed, and decorated the tombs.

A royal foundation, the workmen's village was under the direct supervision of the vizier of the south. In the reign of Ramesses II this was first the vizier Paser, and then his successors Khay, Neferrenpet, and Prahotep. Here, a team of builders and decorators (48 at the beginning of Ramesses's reign, later reduced to 32) was organized according to a naval model: a captain directed two crews, named the crew of the right and the crew of the left (starboard and port), each under the command of a crew chief. These were skilled artists and artisans, perhaps the best in the land, and were for the most part literate. They lived with their families, and some had servants.

L eft: the ruins at Deir
el-Medina run from
the local temple (at left in
the photograph) to the
hill of Qurnet Murai.
The village was reached
by a long central road
and surrounded by a wall
with two gates, at north
and west. Below: a
painted relief portrait of
the vizier Neferrenpet.
The workers of Deir el-
Medina enjoyed a certain
autonomy under the
administrative super-
vision of the vizier. Far
left: the village's small
houses, placed closely
side by side, each com-
prised a string of rooms,
usually a vestibule
housing the domestic

Also living in the village were subordinate
staff, such as water carriers, and two scribes,
who kept the accounting ledgers of the
construction projects and composed official
letters to the authorities. Guards and police
maintained the peace and protected the
work sites.

Much of the village has been excavated,
revealing many details of everyday life in the
time of Ramesses. Written records—stelae,
papyri, and ostraca—have also survived.
Isolated in the desert, the residents raised
donkeys for the transport of water, building
materials, and wares, and small livestock and
fowl for their personal consumption. They
also received provisions from the vizier, or
through the supply office of the reigning pharaoh;
during the reign of Ramesses II this was housed in the
Ramesseum, not far away. The artisans and their families
were supported by the central administration, which
supplied them with fabric, clothing, sandals, firewood,
and other necessities, as well as the tools and materials

divinities, a storage area
for foodstuffs, a main
room whose roof was
supported by a central
column, a bedroom, and
a scullery. A stairway led
to the roof terrace.

for their work, such as the gypsum and colors for the tempera wall paintings in the tombs. Salaries were paid in goods: grains, oil, fats, fish, vegetables, etc.; under Ramesses II, these were occasionally supplemented with meat and wine. The women of the village made bread and beer.

Despite this dependency, the community enjoyed considerable local autonomy. It was governed by an elected council whose composition varied according to the needs of a given time. The council held broad judiciary powers, adjudicating simple disputes and mis-demeanors. Serious crimes were investigated, and then judged by the vizier. The residents of Deir el-Medina also engaged in some trade, exchanging the surplus from their salaries for expensive goods, luxury items, domestic services, and even for personal decora-tions and funerary fittings, products of the talents of their colleagues.

In the written documents we learn much about the

Left: a worker uses an adz in a tomb paint-ing; below: tools from the 18th-Dynasty tomb of Kha at Deir el-Medina. Workers and artisans were buried with their own tools; the tomb of Sennedjem, a contempo-rary of Ramesses II, contained carpenter's squares and plumb lines. A book found at the village's library, called *The Instruction of Khety,* or *The Satire of Trades,* complains of the hardships of manual labor: "Each carpenter who grips an adz is more tired than those who wield a hoe; his fields are the wood and his hoe [to him] is of copper. During the night, when he is free, he still works beyond what his arms can bear; during the night, he burns the candle." This was a text of a type called an Instruction, a collection of maxims and good advice; in this case intended to dissuade students, future scribes, from the manual trades.

family, domestic, religious, professional, social, and economic life of this community, which was especially privileged under Ramesses II. The length and prosperity of his reign allowed an increase in salaries and a decrease in work hours. In 67 years, the workers of Deir el-Medina dug, built, and decorated the final resting places of Ramesses II, his mother, children, daughter-wives, and his wives. Perhaps the most splendid of the tombs from this time is that of Nefertari, in the Valley of the Queens.

During their leisure time, the artisans of the royal tombs built tombs for themselves. Those of Sennedjem, Ipuy, and Pashedu, contemporaneous with Seti I and Ramesses II, are superb examples of a long list of such sepulchers, some of whose ravishing decorations are miraculously preserved.

A passion for the law

The legal affairs of the artisans of Deir el-Medina are preserved in their archives. In this educated milieu, the slightest dispute often gave rise to a legal action, recorded in a succinct text written on either a smooth piece of limestone or a clay potsherd, called an ostracon. Papyrus, an expensive material, was used when the economic stakes were high or the occasion solemn, such as an adoption or a will.

A taste for legal documents and lawsuits was not confined to Deir

Since papyrus was an expensive luxury, artists made sketches, notes, and private artworks on fragments of smooth limestone or on ostraca (potsherds), a material that was abundant and cheap. The manner of these small works is often spontaneous and lively, free from the stylistic conventions that the great royal and public commissions were constrained to follow. Artists used form and space imaginatively, observing postures closely and rendering movement, particularly in scenes of animals. The ostracon was also used for writing accounts, shopping lists, legal notes, and copies of literary and religious texts. A great number of these documents, studies, sketches, and even humorous drawings, some of which illustrate fables, were found at Deir el-Medina. Above: a painted vase; below: an ostracon of an acrobatic dancer.

A beautiful home for the hereafter

The workers of Deir el-Medina placed their own tombs on the slope of the sacred mortuary mountain that faced the hill of Qurnet Murai. These tombs usually comprised a relatively wide, compartmentalized vault and a superstructure with a pyramidion, or small pyramid. Above: a reconstruction drawing. Far left: in a wall painting from his tomb, Inherkau, the foreman of a team, worships the phoenix (in the form of a heron), the bird that rose from the ashes of the dawn on the first morning of the world and is a symbol of eternity. According to the later Greek version of this myth, the phoenix was reborn every 500 or 1,000 years from the ashes of its own funeral pyre. Left: the god Anubis holds in his hands the heart of the deceased, which he is returning to its owner.

Scenes of the afterlife

"The fundamental convention of Egyptian drawing is the simultaneous use of two points of view: plan and elevation. This is done for purposes of explanation and information and, above all, because it is useful in the presentation of objects as primordial, magical personifications. Such figures represent totalities and concepts; they are radically different from those that we understand through the evidence of our senses. In Egypt, only the testimony of the soul is capable of expressing concrete truth in all its facets."

André Lhote,
Chefs-d'oeuvre de la peinture égyptienne,
1954

According to this artistic convention, the bodies of figures were completely visible, with no part hidden behind another. Above left: one tomb-painting tradition depicts scenes from daily life; here, fishermen in their boat, a detail from the tomb of Ipuy. Above right: a scarab, symbol of the future, adorns the tomb of Inherkau. Below: a procession of Pashedu's in-laws, in a stance of adoration, from his tomb.

el-Medina, however. Throughout the empire, troops of lawyers, scribes, and assistants, all under the supervision of the vizier, kept the social system in good working order. Among the well-to-do and the upper bourgeoisie, such disputes were decided by a tribunal. Two interesting records of legal cases illustrate the legal tradition in the New Kingdom period.

The inheritance of Neshi

On one wall of the tomb of Mes, near Memphis, are recorded the particulars of a famous trial that lasted for a century. According to the account of an individual named Nefer and that of the admiral Ahmes, son of Abana, at the beginning of the 18th Dynasty, the pharaoh Ahmose, conqueror of the Hyksos, rewarded his loyal soldiers with land grants. Neshi, an ancestor of Mes, received a parcel of land at this time. He bequeathed the tenure to his children, who, according to a well-established legal custom, worked the fields together, without dividing them. This joint ownership continued for several generations. In the reign of Horemheb, however, a descendant of Neshi who was the eldest heir of the joint owners used legal channels to claim clear title to those parts of the land that she managed, an estate of 13 *arouras,* or 87 acres (35 hectares).

Displeased, a younger sister contested the partition. Each heir then named his or her portion of the land, and a scribe was sent to the sites to record the respective allocations on a cadastre and in the tax ledgers. The eldest sister, assisted by her son, the scribe Huy, then embarked upon a new legal battle to establish her rights. Huy continued to farm his lands until his death, but his widow and their child, a young boy named Mes, were evicted by the other heirs, with the help of a corrupt

Extant letters from ancient Egypt include administrative correspondence between government officials, written in the formulas of the scribal schools, and private letters between friends and relatives. One scribe wrote to his father: "I shall see to it that fifty good *kereshty* breads are brought to you, as the shipper [overcharged] and left only thirty." Above: a letter from the scribe Butehamun to General Payankh.

bureaucrat named Khay. The widow, convinced of her rights, demanded to see the tax registry. She went before the vizier at the royal court of Piramesse, accompanied by Khay and a priest-magistrate named Amenemope, only to find that her son's and husband's names had been erased from the lists.

Khay had devised the affair in order to acquire the land parcel for himself. Mes grew to adulthood with the ownership still in dispute. He became the scribe of the treasury of Ptah at Memphis, and in turn instituted proceedings against Khay, in which he accused him of falsifying the registries. Thanks to the testimony of neighbors and friends, he was able to prove that he was a descendent of Neshi, and that his father had farmed the land in question throughout his life. Thus, in the reign of Ramesses II, the court at Memphis rendered a decision in favor of Mes, who recuperated his estate. He had the scene, with the trial's happy ending and the proof supporting it, inscribed on the wall of the small court adjacent to his tomb.

The inheritance of the scribe Ramose of Deir el-Medina

An official scribe was no mere clerk, but a literate bureaucrat of considerable standing and prosperity. Ramose was first the scribe of the treasury of the funerary temple of Thutmose IV and later elevated by the vizier Paser to the position of scribe of Deir el-Medina, in year 5 of Ramesses's reign. In

"Take a wife while you are still young; she will give you a son and she will bring him into the world while you are still young. It is wise to have children; a man is happy when his children are many, [for] his worth is measured by the number of his descendants." This aphorism from the scribe Any's *Book of the Dead* was popular with the residents of Deir el-Medina, who copied extracts from the text for their own use. Below: Pendua, a worker from Deir el-Medina, and his wife, Nefertary.

this position he accumulated great wealth, which he invested primarily in funerary monuments and sacred objects. Nevertheless, despite his great devotion to the goddess Hathor, and prayers and offerings to the gods and goddesses of fertility, he and his wife were childless. The couple adopted a young boy named Kenherkhepeshef, who eventually succeeded his adoptive father as scribe. Kenherkhepeshef apparently lacked Ramose's finesse and did not hesitate to make the workers and artists of the royal tombs work for him personally, thus earning the disrespect of his employer, the vizier Khay. Nonetheless, he was rich, and when he was in his 50s or 60s, he married an adolescent girl named Naunakhte, but had no children. After his death, the young woman remarried. Much later (under the reign of Ramesses V), when she herself was old, she composed a will, dividing her extensive property among eight of her children (one of whom was a son named Kenherkhepeshef, after her first husband) and disinheriting the others because of their ingratitude. This text was of unusual length for a private document: a costly papyrus measuring 76 inches by 17 inches (192 centimeters by 43 centimeters).

As this papyrus indicates, under Ramesses II—and indeed throughout the pharaonic

Thoth was the scribe god, the Lord of Hieroglyphics, the patron of writers, researchers, and written knowledge. He was credited with the invention of both writing and the law, and it was he who, at the creation of the world, surveyed the land, recorded its dimensions, and distributed it among the cities and *nomes*. Thoth was also master of the calendar and of all things that are counted or measured, including the deeds of the deceased, which he noted on a palette at the time of divine judgment. He was sometimes depicted as an ibis (or an ibis-headed figure), and sometimes as a baboon. As manifestation of divine law, he exercised judicial functions at the side of the goddess Maat, and was the model for earthly judges and kings. Scribes in ancient Egypt were persons of authority and high status. They were active throughout the government, especially in accounting divisions, and were often depicted in artworks under the protection of their patron. Left: Thoth, in baboon form, sits above a scribe at work.

period—women held full and complete legal privileges. Not only could they inherit and bequeath property as Naunakhte had done, but they could also carry out personal transactions, hire servants, train apprentices, draw up wills, and testify in court. Women could manage an inheritance, and even serve as judges on the village councils.

The practice of medicine

Most medical doctors were paid officers of the state and were often trained in a specialty. The clergy of the lioness goddess Sekhmet also practiced human and veterinary medicine. Throughout the ancient world, magic and medicine were closely intertwined, and prescribed remedies were considered to draw their efficacy from magical formulas. For example, a well-known medical papyrus records "words to recite when one applies a medication on whatever sort of ailment of an individual. The efficacy of the remedy will be increased manifold." In the time of Ramesses II, Egyptian doctors and magicians had an international

Above: the scribe Ramose and his wife; below: the pyramidion of his tomb.

"The scribe is deemed a man who listens, and he who listens becomes a man who acts."
The Satire of Trades,
New Kingdom
instructional text

reputation and were esteemed at all the courts of the empire. By the standards of the age their knowledge was considerable, but the powers of their gods were also greatly respected.

A number of extraordinary medical papyri have survived. These indicate that Egyptian doctors knew how to make diagnoses and how to prescribe therapies based upon a substantial knowledge of anatomy. They were skillful in the art of surgery and the empirical use of medications, mainly extracts from animal, vegetable, and mineral products. On the other hand, they did not understand the functions of the organs well.

The name of the goddess Sekhmet, She Who Is Powerful, is derived from *sekhem*. Companion of Ptah at Memphis, the lioness goddess strikes down law-breakers, spreading carnage and plagues. She dispenses suffering, but also healing, and is thus linked to the practice of medicine. Her clergy were magicians and physicians.

Private art in the shadow of pharaonic art

In addition to the professions of lawyer, physician, scribe, priest, and government bureaucrat, artists also flourished under Ramesses II. Not only great lords, but wealthy private citizens built and decorated tombs for themselves and purchased statues and jewelry. While the magnificent, monumental public art commissioned by pharaohs and nobles tended to follow an official, established style, private sculpture and painting were able to display greater individualism. In comparison to the imposing grandeur of the royal statues, paintings, and reliefs, these private artworks could be solemn and austere or ornate and quite mannered. In such private works artists expressed piety in a more personal way, for example. The general prosperity of the times also permitted the use of many colors of paint and precious materials such as fine

marble and gold. Jewelry became heavier and clothing fuller, with a fashion for complicated folds. The quality of execution obviously depended on the financial resources of the owner—which is to say, his or her social rank. In addition to polished paintings and sculptures, modest sketches and spontaneous drawings have survived, some of which have a satirical tone. They fill the modern viewer with wonder at the freshness, tension, and immediacy of their line and color.

Literature

The site at Deir el-Medina has produced an enormous quantity of copies of literary works. Great works of prose and poetry were recorded in papyrus rolls, collected in royal archives and libraries, and displayed in wall inscriptions, but ordinary Egyptians also loved books and many residents of Deir el-Medina had private collections. Since papyrus was expensive, they copied selections of contemporary literature and excerpts from the classics on ostraca, large fragments of ceramic potsherds or flat panels of limestone. Popular ancient texts included educational *Miscellanies* and

The god Anubis invented the technique of embalming. Above: he prepares the corpse of Sennedjem for burial, in a scene painted in Sennedjem's tomb. The primary function of the mummification process was to preserve the body in anticipation of its eventual resurrection, whether literal or mystical. This practice taught Egyptians the principles of anatomy, and very early on enabled them to master the instruments and methods of surgery. Left: a statue of the goddess Sekhmet from Karnak; behind her, a medical treatise discussing the illnesses of the stomach and their remedies.

fictional stories such as *The Tale of Sinuhe*.
Contemporary literature included tales and
legends (*The Tale of the Two Brothers, The
Tale of the Predestined Prince*); histories and
mythological or allegorical fables (*The Tale
of Horus and Set, The Tale of Truth and
Falsehood*); fictions purporting to be histories
(*The Prophetic Tale, The Tale of Seqenenra and*

Above: an ostracon
sketch of a boat,
possibly funerary image.
Many gods, including
some foreign ones, had
cults at Deir el-Medina.
Left: a small private
chapel devoted to three
gods, Khnum, deity of
the First Cataract of the
Nile; Satet, from the
island of Elephantine;
and Anuket. There may
have been a local
sanctuary dedicated to
these three in the village.
The primary god
worshiped there was
Amun, who was revered
in both his official
manifestation and his
animal forms, the goose
and the ram, as well as
through the goddess
Hathor. Ramose, the
scribe of the royal tomb
during the reign of
Ramesses II, built a small
temple to Hathor, which
was endowed by the
Ramesseum. The artisans
also dedicated a cult to
Meretseger, She Loves
Silence, the goddess of
the Theban necropolises,
often personified in the
form of a cobra.

Apepi, The Tale of the Capture of Joppa); and a wide range
of poems, epics, and other narratives. *The Battle of
Qadesh*, a lyrical epic poem, seems to have been fairly
popular in Deir el-Medina. During the 19th Dynasty,
a new literary form gained currency: romantic and
dramatic love poetry, some of which had a semireligious
tone, such as the *Hymn to the Nile Flood*, which enjoyed
great success.

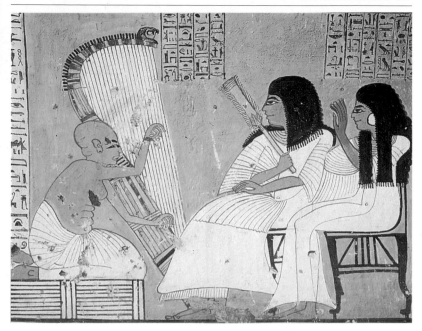

The Ramesseum as cultural center

The Ramesseum, built as the pharaoh's personal mortuary temple at Thebes, was also Ramesses's great foundation of learning and culture. It housed an institution called a House of Life, a cross between a university and a monastery that was home to theologians and scribes who studied and copied mythological and religious texts, hymns to the glory of the gods and the king, and documents concerning ancient rituals. Under Ramesses II, the official religion tended to simplification and syn-

The principal musical instruments in ancient Egypt were the harp, lute, and double flute, which were accompanied by various sorts of timpani—castanets, tambourines, sistra, and *menat* necklaces, whose clicking beads delighted the goddess Hathor. Above: in a wall painting from the tomb of Inherkau, a blind harpist sings for guests at a banquet, urging them to enjoy life. The sage Ptahhotep declared: "Follow your desires throughout all your life!" Left: a woman plays a stringed instrument on an ostracon from Deir el-Medina.

cretism, embracing foreign gods and encouraging the development of a personal relationship between the pharaoh and the gods. Funerary literature was an important genre, and the most important collection of funeral rituals, spells, and texts, *The Book of the Dead* (properly titled *The Spell for Coming Forth by Day*) was widely read. Another such book is *The Book of the Gates*.

Universalism and cosmopolitanism characterized intellectual life under Ramesses II. The House of Life was a school for physicians, magicians, scribes, astronomers, surveyors, architects, geologists, and artists. Encyclopedists classified and recorded vast stores of knowledge by category: birds, fish, and

Animal fables were apparently popular in Egypt, and some were probably the sources for later writers. Aesop's tale of the lion and the rat, for example, was derived from an Egyptian story found in a papyrus from Lower Egypt called the *Myth of the Eye and the Sun*. Left: a scene from a fable; below: a Deir el-Medina ostracon fragment with hieratic writing, a cursive script used by scribes.

plants were catalogued, as were cities, gods, and sets of rules and duties. They produced endless lists of this sort, called *onomastica,* which were sometimes accompanied by a glossary. The Ramesseum undoubtedly housed a great library, which artists from nearby Deir el-Medina consulted to draw inspiration for their works.

The dazzling pharaoh

On the eve of a 30-year jubilee, in approximately 1213 BC, Ramesses II died in Piramesse, his palace city in the eastern Delta. The prescribed rituals for the burial of a pharaoh were elaborate: during a 70-day consecrated period, his body was embalmed. Then,

Above: a panoramic view of Deir el-Medina (left) and the Ramesseum (right). The latter was a complex of buildings that comprised the royal tomb and its priestly cult, and an institution of learning. These roles—scholarly, religious, cultural, and economic—functioned together. Left: this campaniform capital of a column in the hypostyle hall of Ramesses's temple has retained some of its original painted decoration.

A book for the world to come

The Book of the Dead, also called *The Spell for Coming Forth by Day*, was a collection of spells, formulas, and aphorisms, grouped in about 200 chapters of varying length, with illustrations, that instructed a deceased person in how to pass into the realm of the dead, to dwell in a state of bliss. Copies of this text were written on mummy cloths, amulets, or book rolls and placed with a corpse in a tomb. The formulas taught the dead person's spirit how to come and go freely, and how to return from the tomb to enjoy earthly pleasures once again. To achieve this, one had to deserve eternal happiness, winning the sympathy of the gods and triumphing over the infernal powers. The most important scene of this perilous journey was the moment of divine judgment, described in chapter 125 and often illustrated. Here the deceased person stood before the supreme judges of *maat* to plead his or her case, reciting the Declaration of the Innocent (see page 131). Mummification allowed the dead person to remain physically intact for this purpose. Left: a vignette from *The Book of the Dead,* featuring the jackal of Anubis. Overleaf: the god Khnum and the infernal deities.

with great pomp, a grand funeral procession traveled up the Nile until it reached Thebes, where the king was conveyed to his tomb, his eternal home.

It may truthfully be said that the reign of Ramesses II marked a point of culmination in pharaonic history. Under his administration the imperial power of Egypt grew immensely, and the empire greatly extended its international political authority and its cultural and religious influence. The efficiency of his government, the splendor of his court, and the number and importance of his monuments remained unequaled. In his time the land enjoyed a long period of general peace and prosperity.

Merenptah, 13th son and successor

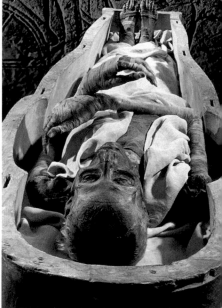

Ramesses II has traveled a good deal since his death, and some of his movements are recorded in a hieratic text inscribed on the lid of his rather simple wooden mummy case (near left). This may not be the original case, and some scholars think it is not that of Ramesses at all. The first tomb of the pharaoh is number 7 in the Valley of the Kings, across the Nile from Luxor. (Above: a view of the valley.) It was vulnerable to grave robbers and in the 21st Dynasty his mummy was moved for safety to the more protected tomb of his father, Seti I. Then it, together with those of many other sovereigns (including Amenhotep I and Seti I), was reburied in the famous hidden cache of Deir el-Bahri. This was discovered in 1871 and the royal mummies were then moved to a museum in Thebes. The mummy is now in the Egyptian Museum in Cairo. Opposite page: the reddish tinge of the king's hair is still discernible. Overleaf: the great king in his open mummy case.

to Ramesses, was able to maintain this level of success for several years, but after him a period of inexorable decline set in and gradually brought the 19th Dynasty to an end in a welter of quarrels over succession, falling standards of living, loss of influence, threats of invasion from without, and corruption from within. The last brilliant reign was that of the second pharaoh of the 20th Dynasty, Ramesses III, who attempted to imitate his illustrious predecessor. But he could not match his ancestor's achievements. Ramesses II remained the exemplar, in deeds and in memory dazzling and incomparable, like the sun at its zenith.

DOCUMENTS

Religious texts

Egyptian religion was polytheistic, with a pantheon of gods, from whom the pharaoh received his divine powers. In the period of Ramesses II, there was a tendency toward simplification and an inclination to embrace gods of foreign cultures that had joined the empire. Among the most important rites were those connected with the afterlife and veneration of the dead; burial customs and their related literature were extensive. Funerary texts such as The Book of the Gates *and* The Book of the Dead *grew very popular.*

Hymn to Amun

This poetic litany is addressed to Amun, the self-created god who initiated the beginning of existence, and who confers legitimacy on the monarchy; the pharaoh is his son and representative on earth, protector of the weak as is the god.

Pilot who knows the water,
Helmsman of [the weak];
Who gives bread to him who has none,
Who nourishes the servant of his house.
I take not a noble as protector,
I associate not with a man of wealth,
I place not my share in another's care,
[My] wealth is in the house of my [lord].
My lord is my protector,
I know his might, to wit:
A helper strong of arm,
None but he is strong.
Amun who knows compassion,
Who hearkens to him who calls him,
Amen-Re, the King of Gods,
The Bull great of strength, who loves strength.

In *Ancient Egyptian Literature:
A Book of Readings,*
translated by Miriam Lichtheim, 1976

The Book of the Dead

The Book of the Dead (*or* The Spell for Coming Forth by Day) *is a collection of formulas or spells, usually written in hieratic script on a papyrus roll that was placed near the deceased in his or her*

Detail of a papyrus manuscript called *The Book of the Dead* of Neferrenpet, 19th Dynasty. Previous page: the gods Horus and Set, symbols of the union of Upper and Lower Egypt, detail of a carving on the socle of the throne of Ramesses II in the temple of Luxor.

tomb. Illustrations or vignettes decorated the principal chapters. The most famous section is chapter 125, known as "The Judgment of the Dead."

THE DECLARATION OF THE INNOCENT

To be said on reaching the Hall of the Two Truths so as to purge N of any sins committed and to see the face of every god:

Hail to you great God, Lord of the
    Two Truths!
I have come to you, my Lord,
I was brought to see your beauty.
I know you, I know the names of the
    forty-two gods,
Who are with you in the Hall of the
    Two Truths,
Who live by warding off evildoers,
Who drink of their blood,
On that day of judging characters
    before Wennofer.
Lo, your name is "He-of-Two-
    Daughters,"
(And) "He-of-Maat's-Two-Eyes."
Lo, I come before you,
Bringing Maat to you,
Having repelled evil for you.

I have not done crimes against
    people,
I have not mistreated cattle,
I have not sinned in the Place of
    Truth.
I have not known what should not
    be known,
I have not done any harm.
I did not begin a day by exacting more
    than my due,
My name did not reach the bark of the
    mighty ruler.
I have not blasphemed a god.
I have not robbed the poor.
I have not done what the god abhors,

I have not maligned a servant to his
    master.
I have not caused pain,
I have not caused tears.
I have not killed,
I have not ordered to kill,
I have not made anyone suffer.
I have not damaged the offerings in
    the temples,
I have not depleted the loaves of the
    gods,
I have not stolen the cakes of the dead.
I have not copulated nor defiled
    myself.
I have not increased nor reduced the
    measure,
I have not diminished the arura,
I have not cheated in the fields.
I have not added to the weight of the
    balance,
I have not falsified the plummet of the
    scales.
I have not taken milk from the mouth
    of children,
I have not deprived cattle of their
    pasture.
I have not snared birds in the reeds of
    the gods,
I have not caught fish in their ponds.
I have not held back water in its
    season,
I have not dammed a flowing stream,
I have not quenched a needed fire.
I have not neglected the days of meat
    offerings.
I have not detained cattle belonging to
    the god,
I have not stopped a god in his
    procession.
I am pure, I am pure, I am pure, I am
    pure!
I am pure as is pure that great heron in
    Hnes.
I am truly the nose of the Lord of
    Breath,

An image from *The Book of the Dead* of Neferrenpet, 19th Dynasty.

Who sustains all the people,
On the day of completing the Eye in
    On,
In the second month of winter, last
    day,
In the presence of the lord of this
    land,
In this Hall of the Two Truths;
For I know the names of the gods in it,
The followers of the great God!
        In *Ancient Egyptian Literature:
        A Book of Readings,*
    translated by Miriam Lichtheim, 1976

Song for Neferhotep

*The belief of the ancient Egyptians in a
life after death included a strong respect
for the memory of the dead, which was
expressed during festivals and banquets.
Through the voice of a singer-harpist,
who by tradition was often blind, the
gathering recalled the deeds of a deceased
person and his or her departure for the
dwelling of the blessed, at the same time
praising the pleasures of life on earth.
This classic example is one of three that
appear in a wall painting, together with a
scene of a banquet, in Theban Tomb 50.*

FIRST SONG
Chanted by the singer with the harp for
the God's Father of Amun, Neferhotep,
vindicated:

O all you excellent eminent dead, O
    Ennead, O Lady of Life in the West,
    hear what has been composed
To sing the praises of the God's Father
    in honoring his soul,
    what is helpful for the excellent dead
    man
Now that he is a living god for eternity,
    elevated in the West.
May these words become a memorial in
    future
    to anyone who passes by.

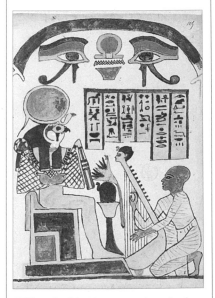

The stele of the Harpist, as redrawn by the archaeologist Jean-François Champollion.

I have heard those songs in the tombs
of ancient days
and what they say, exalting life on
earth and belittling the city of the
dead.
Why is this, acting this way against the
land of eternity
which is just and without terror?
It loathes disorder:
and no one arms himself against a
neighbor in this land without a
rebel.
All our ancestors have come to rest
within it
since the wastes at the beginning of
time;

And those who shall come to be,
millions on millions,
all go there.
There is no lingering in our Beloved
Land,
not one fails to arrive there;
And the span of what was done on
earth is the flicker of a dream
when they say, "Welcome, safe and
sound!" to the one who reaches the
West.

In *Hymns, Prayers, and Songs:
An Anthology of Ancient
Egyptian Lyric Poetry,*
translated by John L. Foster,
1995

The awe-inspiring monumental columns of Ramesses's hypostyle hall at Karnak, richly engraved
with scenes and hieroglyphic texts, tower over human beings.

Political texts

The reign of Ramesses II has bequeathed abundant government documents to us. Diplomatic correspondence, royal decrees, laws and court records, administrative memoranda, public accounts, and the autobiographies of officials constitute a collection that, while certainly incomplete, is sufficient to paint a detailed picture of life and culture at the court of the pharaoh.

The Installation of the Vizier

This remarkable document delineates the manner in which the pharaoh confirms a vizier, and describes the responsibilities that go with the job. The vizier was the chief administrator, the most important person in the realm, after the pharaoh. The tomb of Rekhmira, vizier of Thutmose III (18th Dynasty), displays on its walls a well-preserved version of this text, listing in detail the honors and obligations of the vizier and the scope of his power. Here we read the speech of the pharaoh.

THE SPEECH OF THE PHARAOH
His majesty said to him:
Look to the office of vizier,
Watch over all that is done in it,
Lo, it is the pillar for the whole land.
Lo, being vizier,
Lo, it is not sweet.
Lo, it is bitter as gall.
Lo, he is the copper that shields the
    gold of his master's house,
Lo, he is not one who bends his face to
    magistrates and councillors,
Not one who makes of anyone his
    client.
Lo, what a man does in his master's
    house will be his happiness,
Lo, he shall not act [in the house] of
    another.

Lo, petitioners come from the South
    and the North,
The whole land is eager for [the counsel
    of the vizier];
See to it that all is done according to
    law,
That all is done exactly right,
In [giving a man] his vindication.
Lo, the magistrate who judges in
    public,

Wind and water report all that he does,
Lo, there is none who ignores his deeds.
If he makes [a mistake in deciding] his
case,
And fails to reveal it through the mouth
of the clerk,
It will be known through the mouth
of him whom he judged,
Through his telling it to the clerk by
saying:
"This is not the decision of my case."
If the petitioner is sent—
—— or magistrate,
One will not ignore what he did.
Lo, the magistrate's safety is acting by
the rule,
In acting on a petitioner's speech;
Then the judged [cannot say]:
"I was not given my right."
[A proverb in *The Book of Memphis* says:
"Gracious king, lawful vizier."]

Avoid what was said of the vizier
Akhtoy,
That he denied his own people for the
sake of others,
For fear of being falsely called [partial].
If one of them appealed a judgment,
That he had planned to do to him,
He persisted in denying him,
But that is excess of justice.
Do not judge unfairly,
God abhors partiality;
This is an instruction,
Plan to act accordingly.
Regard one you know like one you
don't know,
One near you like one far from you.
The magistrate who acts like this,
He will succeed here in this place.

Do not pass over a petitioner,
Before you have considered his speech.
When a petitioner is about to petition
you,

A statue of Osiris with crossed flails
discovered in the tomb of the sons of
Ramesses II, Thebes, 19th Dynasty.

Don't dismiss what he says as already
said.
Deny him after you let him hear
On what account you have denied him.
Lo, it is said:
"A petitioner wants his plea considered
Rather than have his case adjudged."
Do not scold a man wrongfully,
Scold where scolding is due.
Cast your fear, that you be feared,
The feared magistrate is a magistrate.
A magistrate's worth is that he does
right,
But if a man makes himself feared a
million times,

People think something is wrong with
him,
And they don't say of him, "He is a
man."

This too is said:
A magistrate who lies comes out as he
deserves.
Lo, you succeed in doing this office by
doing justice,
Lo, doing justice is what is wanted in
the actions of the vizier,
Lo, the vizier is its true guardian since
the time of god.
Lo, what one says of the vizier's chief
scribe:
"Scribe of Justice" one says of him.
As to the hall in which you judge,
It has a room full of [written] decisions.
He who does justice before all people,
He is the vizier.
Lo, a man remains in his office,
If he acts as he is charged,
Innocent is the man who acts as he is
told.
Do not act willfully
In a case where the law is known;
For as regards the headstrong man,
The Lord prefers the timid to the
headstrong man.
Act then in accord with the charge
given you.
Lo, [it is laid upon you].

In *Ancient Egyptian Literature:
A Book of Readings,*
translated by Miriam Lichtheim, 1976

The autobiography of Bakenkhons

*Ramesses II favored the cult of Amun,
and under his rule the temple and its
priesthood rapidly grew to dizzying
heights of religious, economic, and
political power. The temple's high priest
was thus a key figure in public life.
Bakenkhons was one of a class of high*

*officials, personally loyal to the king, with
whom Ramesses II surrounded himself.
This high priest, who was also a royal
architect, had a long inscription placed on
a statue of himself to describe his long
career. Here is a passage from it.*

I was a good father to my subordinates,
fostering their young people, giving a
hand to anyone in need, maintaining
alive the poverty-stricken, performing
good deeds in [Amun's] temple. I built
for him the Temple Ramesses-II-Who-
Hears-Prayer, at the Upper Gateway of
the Temple of Amun. I erected in it
granite obelisks whose beauty reached
the heavens, before them a portico
opposite the town of Thebes, and
basins and gardens planted with trees.
I made two very great door-leaves
[plated] with electrum that reflected the
sky. I made two very great flag-staffs,
and erected them in the forecourt
before his temple. I constructed great
river-barges for Amun, Mut and
Khons.

From K. A. Kitchen,
*Pharaoh Triumphant:
The Life and Times of Ramesses II,
King of Egypt,* 1982

The Egyptian–Hittite treaty

*The peace accord concluded between
Ramesses II and Hattusilis [Hattusil] III,
ruler of the Hittites, in year 21 of the
former's reign is of exceptional interest,
as it constitutes the first known written
treaty between two sovereign states. It
put an end to a long period of conflict
between Egypt and Hatti for control of
Syria and the Phoenician cities, allowing
both empires to turn their attention
to threats from Libya and Assyria,
respectively. It thus marked the beginning
of a long peace, and may indeed be*

The Hittite version of the Egyptian–Hittite treaty, written in cuneiform.

considered a founding text on international political rights. Here is the version written by the Hittites and sent to Egypt:

Now as regards the time of Muwatallis the Great Ruler of Hatti, my brother, he fought with [Ramesses II], the Great Ruler of Egypt. But now, as from today, behold Hattusil…[makes] a treaty to establish the relationship which Re made and which Seth made—the land of Egypt with the land of Hatti—to prevent hostilities arising between them, forever.

Behold Hattusil III…binds himself by treaty to Ramesses II…beginning from today, in order to create peace and good brotherhood between us forever—he being friendly and at peace with me, and I being friendly and at peace with him, forever…

The Great Ruler of Hatti shall never trespass against the land of Egypt, to take anything from it. Ramesses II… shall never trespass against the land of Hatti, to take anything from it.

As for the standing treaty which was current in the time of Suppiluliuma [I],… likewise the standing treaty which existed in the time of Muwatallis,…I now adhere to it.

Behold, Ramesses II…[also] adheres to it. The peace which has become ours together, beginning from today, we adhere to it and we shall act in accord with this regular relationship.

If some other foe should come against the territories of Ramesses II…, and he sends word to the Great Ruler of Hatti, saying, 'Come with me as ally against him!'—then the Great Ruler of Hatti shall act [with him, and] shall slay his foes. But if the Great Ruler of Hatti is not disposed to go [personally], then he shall send his troops and chariotry and they shall slay his foes…' And so reciprocally, Ramesses II for Hattusil.

If an Egyptian, or two, or three, shall flee, and they come to the Great Ruler of Hatti, then the Great Ruler of Hatti shall seize them and have them brought back to Ramesses II, Great Ruler of Egypt. As for the person handed back to Ramesses II, Great Ruler of Egypt, let not his error be charged against him, let not his house, his wives or his children be destroyed, and let him not be killed. Let there be no injury [done] to his eyes or his ears, his mouth or his legs. [In fact], let no crime be charged against him....

and similarly in the other direction, in the paragraph that followed:

Now as for these terms of the treaty which the Great Ruler of Hatti has made with Ramesses II, the Great Ruler of Egypt, they are written upon this silver tablet.

As for these terms, a thousand gods of the deities male and female who belong to Hatti, together with a thousand gods of the deities male and female who belong to Egypt—they are with me as witnesses, and they have heard these terms. [Namely]:—

The Sun-god, Lord of Heaven, the Sun-god[dess] of the city Arinna; the Storm-god, Lord of Heaven, the Storm-god of Hatti,...of Arinna; the Storm-gods of Zippalanda, Pittiyarik, Hissaspa, Saressa, Aleppo...; Astarte of the Hatti-land,...the Lady of Karahna, the Lady of the Battlefield, the Lady of Nineveh;...the Queen of Heaven; the gods, the Lords of the Oath;...the Rivers of Hatti-land; the gods of Kizzuwatna.

Amun, Re and Seth; the gods male and female; the streams and mountains of the land of Egypt. Heaven; Earth; the Great Sea; the Wind; the Storm-clouds.

Concerning these terms on this silver tablet for Hatti and for Egypt:—

As for him who does not keep them, the thousand gods of Hatti together with the thousand gods of Egypt shall destroy his house, his land and his servants.

As for him who shall keep these terms [written] on this silver tablet, Hittites or Egyptians,...the thousand gods of Hatti and the thousand gods of Egypt will cause him to flourish, will make him to live, together with his household, his land and his servants.

From K. A. Kitchen,
*Pharaoh Triumphant:
The Life and Times of Ramesses II,
King of Egypt,* 1982

Below and opposite: views of tomb KV7, the Theban tomb in the Valley of the Kings in which Ramesses II was originally buried.

Above: a lithograph by David Roberts from c. 1836 shows the interior of the entrance hall of the temple at Abu Simbel as it looked not long after its rediscovery in 1813.

Below: the original tomb of Ramesses II, KV7, is unfortunately in very bad condition and full of debris, due to floods.

Secular literature

Some stories from the Middle Kingdom, such as The Tale of Sinuhe, *remained popular in the Ramesside period and were tirelessly copied by scribes. Secular literature in Ramesses's time also began to reveal a certain taste for the romantic. Love poetry expressing delight in nature and the exaltation of beautiful sentiments became fashionable. Historical narratives also began to appear, especially accounts of the important events of the pharaoh's long reign. Poets and writers found inspiration, for example, in recounting the splendors of the wedding of Ramesses to the Hittite princess Manefrure.*

Love poetry

19th-Dynasty love songs expressed refined sentiments for an aristocratic audience. Some of these use styles and expressions that resemble those of the biblical Song of Songs. *Here are some poems from a manuscript known as the* Papyrus Harris.

I fare north in the ferry
By the oarsman's stroke,
On my shoulder my bundle of reeds;
I am going to Memphis
To tell Ptah, Lord of Truth:
Give me my sister tonight!
The river is as if of wine,
Its rushes are Ptah,
Sakhmet is its foliage,
Iadet its buds,
Nefertem its lotus blossoms.
[The Golden] is in joy
When earth brightens in her beauty;
Memphis is a bowl of fruit
Placed before the fair-of-face!

I shall lie down at home
And pretend to be ill;
Then enter the neighbors to see me,
Then comes my sister with them.
She will make the physicians unneeded,
She understands my illness!

The voice of the wild goose shrills,

A text written on an ostracon.

A fragment of the *Hymn to the Nile Flood.*

It is caught by its bait;
My love of you pervades me,
I cannot loosen it.
I shall retrieve my nets,
But what do I tell my mother,
To whom I go daily,
Laden with bird catch?
I have spread no snares today,
I am caught in my love of you!

The wild goose soars and swoops,
It alights on the net;
Many birds swarm about,
I have work to do.
I am held fast by my love,
Alone, my heart meets your heart,
From your beauty I'll not part!

The voice of the dove is calling,
It says: "It's day! Where are you?"
O bird, stop scolding me!
I found my brother on his bed,
My heart was overjoyed;

Each said: "I shall not leave you,
My hand is in your hand;
You and I shall wander
In all the places fair."
He makes me the foremost of
women,
He does not aggrieve my heart.

My gaze is fixed on the garden
gate,
My brother will come to me;
Eyes on the road, ears straining,
I wait for him who neglects me.
I made my brother's love my sole
concern,
About him my heart is not silent;
It sends me a fleet-footed messenger
Who comes and goes to tell me:
"He deceives you, in other words,
He found another woman,
She is dazzling to his eyes."
Why vex another's heart to death?

My heart thought of my love of you
When half of my hair was braided;
I came at a run to find you,

And neglected my hairdo.
Now if you let me braid my hair,
I shall be ready in a moment.

                    In *Ancient Egyptian Literature:*
                            A Book of Readings,
            translated by Miriam Lichtheim, 1976

Hymn to the Nile Flood

*The beneficial seasonal floods of the Nile
River were deified under the name of
Hapy. A great lyrical work, composed
during the 19th Dynasty, glorifies this
natural phenomenon, which reliably
occurred at the same time every year,
bringing to the land its legendary fertility.
These are a few passages from it.*

I

May your countenance shine on us,
    Hapy, god of the moving River,
    who comes forth from earth
    returning to save the Black Land.
His features are hidden, dark in the
    daylight,
    yet the faithful find him fit subject
    for song.
He waters the landscape the Sun god
    has formed,
    giving life to every small creature,
Assuaging even the thirsty hills, far
    from the water's edge—
    for his is the rain, as it falls from
    heaven;
Loved by the waiting Earth, he nurtures
    the newborn Grain,
    and crafts of the Fashioner flourish in
    Egypt.

II

Lord of the fish, he sends wildfowl
    flying south,
    and no bird falls prey to the
    stormwind;
He fathers the barley, brings emmer
    to be,

fills the gods' temples with odor of
    festival.
But let him be backward, then
    breathing falters,
    all faces grow fierce with privation;
Should the gods' primal shrines lie dry
    in the dust,
    men by the millions were lost to
    mankind.

III

Absent, he unleashes greed to ravage
    the face of the land—
    famous and small wander homeless
    on highways;
And he baffles mankind as to when he
    draws near, for wayward he is, since
    the day Khnum made him.
Yet when sparkling he rises, the land
    stands rejoicing,
    every belly is filled with elation,
Bones of the creatures are shaken by
    laughter,
    teeth gleam, bared by welcoming
    smiles.

IV

Food bringer, rich with provisions,
    himself the author of all his good
    things,
Awe-striking master, yet sweet the
    aromas rising about him,
    and, how he satisfies when he
    returns!—
Transforming the dust to pastures for
    cattle,
    bringing forth for each god his
    sacrifice.
He dwells in the underworld, yet heaven
    and earth are his to command,
    and the Two Lands he takes for his
    own,
Filling the storerooms, heaping the
    grainsheds,
    giving his gifts to the poor.

V
He causes each kind of good wood to
  grow tall,
  and no one in Egypt lacks timber,
Making the ship move through force of
  his flow,
  so it will not settle like stone.
Yet bluffs are borne off by his fierce
  upsurging,
  while he himself is not seen;
He goes to his work, and will not be
  governed
  though they chant out the secret
  spells;
Man cannot know the place where
  he is,
  nor his grotto be spied in the
  writings.

VI
Flood undercuts village rises, dykes will
  not hold,
  sight wanders, confused, with no
  landmarks to guide it.
Yet hordes of the young join his
  following,
  they hail him as sovereign lord,
For he anchors the earthly rhythms,
  returning in his due season,
  reclaiming the Twin Lands of Sedge
  and Papyri:
Each eye shines with moisture by
  means of him,
  all are rich through his flooding
  kindness.

VII
Poised for his entrance, he rushes forth
  gladly,
  and each stranded heart floats on
  joy.
It was he begot Sobek, son of the Lady
  of Waters
  (how blessed indeed the Great Nine
  he fathered!)—

He foams across fields, sails over his
  marshland,
  impregnating earth for all men;
Yet he makes one strong while stripping
  another,
  nor can judgment be rendered
  against him;
He serves his own altars, refuses the
  time-honored rituals,
  endows for himself no gleaming
  stone temple.

VIII
He illumines those who go forth in
  darkness—
  lighting their way with tallow of
  cattle;
The loom of events, it is his Power
  weaving,
  and no nome of the living lacks him.
He has clothed men with flax since first
  it was sown,
  affording Hedj-hetep help with his
  tasks,
Brewing resins and oils for the god of
  orchards
  so Ptah will have glues to fasten
  things tight;
He readies works of the field for Khepri
  to rise upon—
  there are workers themselves only
  because of him;
All writing belongs to the Word of
  God,
  and he it was supplied the papyri.

IX
He descends to the netherworld, rises
  again,
  Revealer, returning with news of the
  Mysteries;
But if listless he lies, his subjects
  are few—
  he kills them by letting the green
  world wither.

Then no better than women see
Thebans,
    each man in despair destroying his
    gear:
No raw goods for finishing handwork,
    no cloth for the weaving of clothes,
No decking out offspring of rich men,
    no shadowing beautiful eyes,
For lack of him, the trees all in ruins—
    no perfumes to linger on anyone.

X

He plants a sense of due Order deep in
the hearts of mankind,
    lest men forswear the helpless among
    them;
In perfect accord he joins with the
Great Green Sea
    nor seeks to control the sweep of its
    waters;
He offers each god due praise and
worship
    while letting no bird fall to his desert.
There is no grasping of his hand after
gold—
    for no man slakes thirst drinking
    money,
One cannot eat precious stone and be
nourished—
    food first, let prosperity follow.

XI

Songs to the harp are begun for him,
    chanters and singers clap hands,
Troops of the young shout for joy to
him,
    the irrepressible crowd is arrayed:
For he comes! bringing riches,
    burnishing bright the dull land,
    renewing the color and flesh of
    mankind,
Fostering dreams of women with
child,
    wanting hosts of the whole world
    of creatures.

XII

When godlike he shines amid hungry
townsmen,
    by his fruits of the field are they
    satisfied.
He provides for the lotus its new show
of blossoms,
    and all that feeds green things
    overflows earth;
The pastures are crowded with
children—
    they have forgotten how hungry they
    were;
Good streams through the streets and
squares,
    the length of the land frisks and
    flowers.

XIII

Hapy rides high, and thanksgiving is
offered him:
    for him longhorned cattle are
    slaughtered,
For him the festival meal prepared,
    fowl are made fat for him,
Lions trapped out on the desert,
    debts of kindness repaid him;
And to each god they make offering
    just as is done for Hapy:
Incense, birds, beasts big and small—
    all are given;
    and down in his cave Hapy stirs,
    irresistible.
Yet not in the underworld shall his
name be known,
    nor can the very gods reveal it.

XIV

All men honor the Nine Great Gods,
    but They stand in awe of that
    deity
Who aids his son, divine Lord of All,
    in greening the banks of the Nile.
O hidden god, be it well with you! may
    you flourish, and return!

Hapy, river-spirit, may you flourish
and return!
Come back to Egypt, bringing your
benediction of peace,
greening the banks of the Nile;
Save mankind and the creatures, make
life likely,
through the gift of all this your
countryside!
O hidden god, be it well with you! may
you flourish, and return!
Hapy, Lord of Egypt, may you
flourish and return!

In *Echoes of Egyptian Voices:
An Anthology of Ancient
Egyptian Poetry,*
translated by John L. Foster, 1992

The Bentrech stele

*Incised on a stele now in the Musée du
Louvre in Paris is a tale inspired by the
marriage of Ramesses II to the Hittite
Manefrure—an event that struck the
popular imagination deeply. The story
presents the king of Bakhtan, who asks
Ramesses II, his famous son-in-law, to
send an Egyptian doctor to cure his
youngest daughter. Arriving at this
distant court, the doctor certifies that the
young girl is possessed by a spirit that only
the god Khons, He Who Rules in Thebes,
will know how to exorcize.*

His Majesty commanded that
Khonsu who rules destinies in Thebes
should be sent on a great bark escorted
by five smaller boats, by chariots, and
many horses marching on the right
and on the left. When this god arrived
at Bakhtan, in the space of a year and
five months, behold the prince of
Bakhtan came with his soldiers and his
generals before Khonsu who rules
destinies, and threw himself on his
belly, saying, "Thou comest to us, thou
dost join with us, according to the
orders of the king of the two Egypts,
Uasimariya-Satapanriya." Behold as
soon as the god had gone to the place
where Bintrashit was, and had made
the magic passes for the daughter of the
prince of Bakhtan, she became well
immediately, and the spirit who was
with her said in presence of Khonsu
who rules destinies in Thebes, "Come
in peace, great god who drives away
foreigners, Bakhtan is thy town, its
people are thy slaves, and I myself, I am
thy slave. I will go, therefore, to the
place from whence I came, in order to
give satisfaction to thy heart on account
of the matter which brings thee, but
let Thy Majesty command that a feast
day be celebrated for me and for the
prince of Bakhtan." The god made an
approving nod of the head to his
prophet, to say, "Let the prince of
Bakhtan make a great offering before
this ghost." Now, while this was
happening between Khonsu, who rules
destinies in Thebes, and the spirit, the
prince of Bakhtan was there with his
army stricken with terror. And when
they had made a great offering before
Khonsu who rules destinies in Thebes,
and before the ghost, from the prince
of Bakhtan, while celebrating a feast
day in their honour, the spirit departed
in peace whithersoever it pleased him,
according to the command of Khonsu
who rules destinies in Thebes.

The prince of Bakhtan rejoiced
greatly, as well as all the people of
Bakhtan, and he communed with his
heart, saying, "Since this god has been
given to Bakhtan, I will not send him
back to Egypt."

From Gaston Maspéro,
Popular Stories of Ancient Egypt,
translated by A. S. Johns, 1967

The legend of Ramesses

From the time of antiquity, the great pharaoh called Ozymandias, Osymandyas, Sesostris, Sesoösis, Ramses, or Rhamses was enveloped in an enduring legend. His successors in ancient Greece and Rome wrote of his reign as a golden age.

The temple at Abu Simbel, soon after its rediscovery, in an 1819 watercolor by Linant de Bellefonds.

The great Sesostris

The pharaoh referred to in Herodotus's History *as Sesostris is generally presumed to be Ramesses II. This 5th-century BC Greek author from Asia Minor traveled in Egypt and was much impressed by its legends and monuments.*

Sesostris found work, as I shall show, for the multitude which he brought with him from the countries which he had subdued. It was these who dragged the great and long blocks of stone which were brought in this king's reign to the temple of Hephaestus; and it was they who were compelled to dig all the canals which are now in Egypt.... The reason why the king thus intersected the country was this: those Egyptians whose towns were not on the Nile but inland from it lacked water whenever the flood left their land, and drank only brackish water from wells....

This king moreover (so they said) divided the country among all the Egyptians by giving each an equal square parcel of land, and made this his source of revenue, appointing the payment of a yearly tax. And any man who was robbed by the river of a part of his land would come to Sesostris and declare what had befallen him; then the king would send men to look into it and measure the space by which the land was diminished, so that thereafter it should pay in proportion to the tax originally imposed....

Sesostris was the only Egyptian king who also ruled Ethiopia. To commemorate his name, he set before the temple of Hephaestus two stone statues of himself and his wife, each thirty cubits high, and statues of his four sons, each of twenty cubits. Long afterwards Darius the Persian would have set up

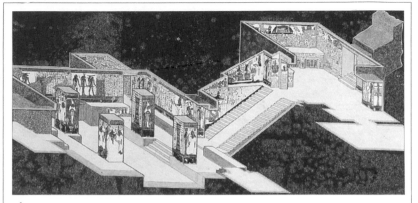

An axonometric drawing of the tomb of Nefertari in the Valley of the Queens.

his statue before these; but the priest of Hephaestus forbade him, saying that he had achieved nothing equal to the deeds of Sesostris the Egyptian.

Herodotus, *The Histories,*
Book II, 108–10,
translated by A. D. Godley, 1975

Egypt was filled to overflowing with benefits

The 1st-century BC Sicilian historian Diodorus was also dazzled.

Sesoösis [Ramesses], they say,... performed more renowned and greater deeds than did any of his predecessors.... Now at the birth of Sesoösis his father did a thing worthy of a great man and a king: Gathering together from over all Egypt the male children which had been born on the same day and assigning to them nurses and guardians, he prescribed the same training and education for them all, on the theory that those who had been reared in the closest companionship and had enjoyed the same frank relationship would be most loyal and as fellow-combatants in the wars most brave. He amply provided for their every need and then trained the youths by unremitting exercises and hardships; for no one of them was allowed to have anything to eat unless he had first run one hundred and eighty stades [about 20 miles, or 34 km]. Consequently upon attaining to manhood they were all veritable athletes of robustness of body, and in spirit qualified for leadership....

First of all Sesoösis, his companions also accompanying him, was sent by his father with an army into Arabia, where he was subjected to the laborious training of hunting wild animals and, after hardening himself to the privations of thirst and hunger, conquered the entire nation of the Arabs, which had never been enslaved before his day; and then, on being sent to the regions to the west, he subdued the larger part of Libya, though in years still no more than a youth. And when he ascended the throne upon the death of his father, being filled with confidence by reason of his earlier exploits he undertook to conquer the inhabited earth. There are those who say that he was urged to acquire empire over the whole world by his own daughter Athyrtis, who, according to some, was far more intelligent than any of her day and showed her father that the campaign would be an easy one....

In preparation for this undertaking he first of all confirmed the goodwill of all the Egyptians towards himself, feeling it to be necessary, if he were to bring his plan to a successful end, that his soldiers on the campaign should be ready to die for their leaders, and that those left behind in their native lands should not rise in revolt. He therefore showed kindnesses to everyone by all means at his disposal, winning over some by presents of money, others by gifts of land, and others by remission of penalties, and the entire people he attached to himself by his friendly intercourse and kindly ways.... And dividing the entire land into thirty-six parts which the Egyptians call nomes, he set over each a nomarch, who should superintend the

The colossal statue of Ramesses II lying in the ruins of the Ramesseum.

collection of the royal revenues and administer all the affairs of his division. He then chose out the strongest of the men and formed an army worthy of the greatness of his undertaking; for he enlisted six hundred thousand foot-soldiers, twenty-four thousand cavalry, and twenty-seven thousand war chariots....

After he had made ready his army he marched first of all against the Ethiopians who dwell south of Egypt, and after conquering them he forced that people to pay a tribute in ebony, gold and the tusks of elephants. Then he sent out a fleet of four hundred ships into the Red Sea [the Persian Gulf], being the first Egyptian to build warships, and not only took possession of the islands in those waters, but also subdued the coast of the mainland as far as India, while he himself made his way by land with his army and subdued all Asia.... He dealt gently with all conquered people and, after concluding his campaign in nine years, commanded the nations to bring presents each year to Egypt according to their ability, while he himself, assembling a multitude of captives which has never been surpassed and a mass of other booty, returned to his country, having accomplished the greatest deeds of any king of Egypt to his day. All the temples of Egypt, moreover, he adorned with notable votive offerings and spoils, and honoured with gifts according to his merits every soldier who had distinguished himself for bravery. And in general, as a result of this campaign not only did the army, which had bravely shared in the deeds of the king and had gathered great wealth, make a brilliant homeward journey, but it also came to pass that all Egypt was filled to overflowing with benefits of every kind.

Sesoösis now relieved his peoples of the labours of war and granted to the comrades who had bravely shared in his deeds a care-free life in the enjoyment of the good things which they had won, while he himself, being ambitious for glory and intent upon everlasting fame, constructed works which were great and marvellous in their conception as well as in the lavishness with which their cost was provided, winning in this way immortal glory for himself and for the Egyptians security combined with ease for all time. For beginning with the gods first, he built in each city of Egypt a temple to the god who was held in special reverence by its inhabitants. On these labours he used no Egyptians, but constructed them all by the hands of his captives alone; and for this reason he placed an inscription on every temple to the effect that no native had toiled upon it....

Now Sesoösis threw up many great mounds of earth and moved to them such cities as happened to be situated on ground that was not naturally elevated, in order that at the time of the flooding of the river both the inhabitants and their herds might have a safe place of retreat. And over the entire land from Memphis to the sea he dug frequent canals leading from the river, his purpose being that the people might carry out the harvesting of their crops quickly and easily, and that, through the constant intercourse of the peasants with one another, every district might enjoy both an easy livelihood and a great abundance of all things which minister to man's enjoyment. The greatest result of this work, however, was that he made the country secure and difficult of access against attacks by enemies; for practically all the best part of Egypt, which before this time had been easy of passage for horses and carts, has from that time on been very difficult for an enemy to invade by reason of the great number of canals leading from the river. He also fortified with a wall the side of Egypt which faces east, as a defence against inroads from Syria and Arabia; the wall extended through the desert from Pelusium to Heliopolis, and its length was some fifteen hundred stades. Moreover, he also built a ship of cedar wood, which was two hundred and eighty cubits long and plated on the exterior with gold and on the interior with silver. This ship he presented as a votive offering to the god who is held in special reverence in Thebes, as well as two obelisks of hard stone one hundred and twenty cubits high, upon which he inscribed the magnitude of his army, the multitude of his revenues, and the number of the peoples he had subdued; also in Memphis in the temples of Hephaestus he dedicated monolithic statues of himself and of his wife, thirty cubits high....

This king is thought to have surpassed all former rulers in power and military exploits, and also in the magnitude and number of the votive offerings and public works which he built in Egypt. And after a reign of thirty-three years he deliberately took his own life, his eyesight having failed him; and this act won for him the admiration not only of the priests of Egypt but of the other inhabitants as well, for it was thought that he had caused the end of his life to comport with the loftiness of spirit shown in his achievements.

Diodorus of Sicily [Diodorus Siculus, *The Library of History*], Book I, 1st century BC, trans. by C. H. Oldfather, 1933

Further Reading

Recent decades have seen the publication of excellent popular scientific works on Ramesses II, particularly those of Kenneth A. Kitchen, Christiane Desroches Noblecourt, and Claire Lalouette.

GENERAL WORKS ON ANCIENT EGYPT

Aldred, C., *The Egyptians*, 1998.

Andrews, C. A. R., *Egyptian Mummies*, 1984.

Baines, J., and Malek, J., *Atlas of Ancient Egypt*, 1979.

Bierbrier, M., *The Tomb-Builders of the Pharaohs*, 1982.

Bjorkman, G., *Kings at Karnak: A Study of the Treatment of the Monuments of Royal Predecessors in the Early New Kingdom*, 1971.

Breasted, J. H., *A History of Egypt, from the Earliest Times to the Persian Conquest*, 1912.

————, *Ancient Records of Egypt*, 5 vols., 1906–7.

Bucaille, M., *Mummies of the Pharaohs: Modern Medical Investigations*, trans. A. D. Pannell and the author, 1990.

Budge, E. A. W., *The Dwellers on the Nile*, 1992.

Cambridge Ancient History, Part II, vol. 2A, 1975.

Černy, J., *Paper and Books in Ancient Egypt*, 1953.

Champollion, J.-F., *Monuments de l'Egypte et de la Nubie*, 1845.

Clark, R. T. Rundle,

Myth and Symbol in Ancient Egypt, 1978.

Clayton, P. A., *Chronicle of the Pharaohs: The Reign-by-Reign Record of the Rulers and Dynasties of Ancient Egypt*, 1994.

Davies, N. M., *Ancient Egyptian Paintings*, ed. A. H. Gardiner, 1936.

Davies, W. V., *Egyptian Hieroglyphs*, 1987.

Desroches Noblecourt, C., *Ancient Egypt: The New Kingdom and the Amarna Period*, 1960.

————, *Egyptian Wall Paintings from Tombs and Temples*, UNESCO, 1962.

————, *The Great Pharaoh Ramses II and His Time: An Exhibition of Antiquities from the Egyptian Museum, Cairo*, trans. E. Mialon, 1985.

El Mahdy, C., *Mummies, Myth, and Magic in Ancient Egypt*, 1989.

Galan, J. M., *Victory and Border: Terminology Related to Egyptian Imperialism in the XVIIIth Dynasty*, 1995.

Gardiner, A. H., *Egypt of the Pharaohs: An Introduction*, 1961.

Goedicke, H., and Roberts, J. J. M., *Unity and Diversity: Essays in the History, Literature, and Religion of the Ancient Near East*, 1975.

Grandet, P., *Contes de l'Egypte ancienne*, 1998.

Grimal, N., *Histoire de l'Egypte ancienne*, 1988.

Harrison, R. K., *Major Cities of the Biblical World*, 1985.

Hart, G., *A Dictionary of Egyptian Gods and Goddesses*, 1986.

————, *Egyptian Myths*, 1990.

Hornung, E., *Conceptions of God in Ancient Egypt*, 1983.

————, *The Valley of the Kings*, 1990.

James, T. G. H., *Pharaoh's People: Scenes from Life in Imperial Egypt*, 1984.

Janssen, J. and R., *Growing Up in Ancient Egypt*, 1991.

Kemp, B. J., *Ancient Egypt: Anatomy of a Civilization*, 1989.

Knapp, A. B., *The History and Culture of Ancient Western Asia and Egypt*, 1988.

Lhote, A., *Chefs-d'oeuvre de la peinture égyptienne*, 1954.

Lucas, A., *Ancient Egyptian Materials and Industries*, 4th ed., rev. by J. P. Harris, 1962.

Maspéro, G., *Manual of Egyptian Archaeology and Guide to the Study of Antiquities in Egypt*, trans. A. B. Edwards, 1902.

Menu, B., ed., "Egypte pharaonique: pouvoir, société," *Méditerranées*, 1996.

Morenz, S., *Egyptian Religion*, 1983.

Murnane, W. J., *The Penguin Guide to Ancient Egypt*, 1983.

Newby, P. H., *The Warrior Pharaohs*, 1980.

O'Connor, D., and Silverman, D. P., eds.,

Ancient Egyptian Kingship, 1995.

Partridge, R. B., *Faces of the Pharaohs: Royal Mummies and Coffins from Ancient Thebes*, 1994.

Quirke, S., *Who Were the Pharaohs?: A History of Their Names with a List of Cartouches*, 1990.

Quirke, S., and Spencer, J., eds., *The British Museum Book of Ancient Egypt*, 1992.

Redford, D. B., *Egypt, Canaan, and Israel in Ancient Times*, 1992.

Rose, J., *The Sons of Re: Cartouches of the Kings of Egypt*, 1985.

Sauneron, S., *The Priests of Ancient Egypt*, 1960, 1969.

Shaw, I., and Nicholson, P., *The Dictionary of Ancient Egypt*, 1995.

Strouhal, E., *Life of the Ancient Egyptians*, 1992.

Taylor, J. H., *Egypt and Nubia*, 1991.

Tiradritti, F., ed., *Egyptian Treasures from the Egyptian Museum in Cairo*, 1999.

Trigger, B., *Nubia and the Pharaohs*, 1978.

Trigger, B., et al., *Ancient Egypt: A Social History*, 1983.

Vandersleyen, C., *L'Egypte et la vallée du Nil*, vol. 2: *De la fin de l'Ancien Empire à la fin du Nouvel Empire*, 1995.

Vercoutter, J., *The Search for Ancient Egypt*, 1992.

————, *L'Egypte et la vallée du Nil*, vol. 1: *Des*

origines à la fin de l'Ancien Empire, 1992.

ANCIENT TEXTS

Allam, S., *Hieratische Ostraka und Papyri aus Ramessidenzeit*, 1973.

Barucq, A., and Daumas, F., *Hymnes et prières de l'Egypte ancienne*, 1980.

Diodorus of Sicily, Books I and II, trans. C. H. Oldfather, 1933.

Edel, E., ed., *Die Ägyptisch-hethitische Korrespondenz aus Boghazkoi in babylonischer und hethitischer Sprache*, 1994.

The Egyptian Book of the Dead: The Book of Going Forth by Day, Being the Papyrus of Ani, trans. R. O. Faulkner, 1994.

Faulkner, R. O., *The Ancient Egyptian Book of the Dead*, rev. ed. by C. A. R. Andrews, 1990.

Gray, T., "And in the Tombs Were Found…," *Plays and Portraits of Old Egypt*, 1923.

Kitchen, K. A., *Ramesside Inscriptions, Historical and Biographical*, vols. 1–8, 1969–90.

Lalouette, C., *Textes sacrés et textes profanes de l'ancienne Egypte*, 2 vols., 1987.

Lefebvre, G., *Romans et contes egyptiens de l'époque pharaonique*, 1949, repr. 1976.

Lichtheim, M., *Ancient Egyptian Literature*, 2 vols., 1973–80.

Murphy, E., ed. and trans., *The Antiquities of Egypt, A Translation with Notes of Book I of the "Library of History" of Diodorus Siculus*, 1990.

Parkinson, R. B., *Voices from Ancient Egypt*, 1991.

Simpson, W. K., Faulkner, R. O., and Wente, E., *The Literature of Ancient Egypt*, 1972.

ON RAMESSES II

Birch, S., "Upon an Historical Tablet of Ramesses II, 19th Dynasty, Relating to the Gold Mines of Aethiopia," *Archaeologia* 34, 1852.

Desroches Noblecourt, C., *Ramsès II: La Véritable histoire*, 1996.

Freed, R. E., *Ramesses the Great: His Life and World*, 1987.

Graetz, K. S., ed., and Griggs, C. W., *Ramses II: The Pharaoh and His Time*, exh. cat., 1985

Le Grand Pharaon Ramsès II et son temps, exh. cat., 1985.

Kitchen, K. A., *Pharaoh Triumphant: The Life and Times of Ramesses II, King of Egypt*, 1982.

Lalouette, C., *L'Empire des Ramsès*, 1985.

Schmidt, J. D., *Ramesses II: A Chronological Structure of His Reign*, 1973.

Velikovsky, I., *Ramses II and His Time*, 1978.

SPECIALIZED WORKS

Allam, S., "Aspects de la vie sociale, juridique et municipale à Deir el-Médineh," *Méditerranées* 6/7, 1996.

Balout, L., et al., *La Momie de Ramsès: Contribution scientifique à l'Egyptologie*, 1985.

Černy, J., "Prices and Wages in Egypt in the Ramesside Period," *Cahiers d'histoire mondiale* I, 1953–54.

Desroches Noblecourt, C., and Kuentz, C., *Le Petit Temple d'Abou Simbel I*, 1968.

Eyre, C.-J., "Ordre et désordre dans la campagne égyptienne," *Méditerranées* 6/7, 1996.

Forman, W., and Quirke, S., *Hieroglyphs and the Afterlife in Ancient Egypt*, 1996.

Gardiner, A. H., *The Kadesh Inscriptions of Ramesses II*, 1960.

———, *Ramesside Administrative Documents*, 1948.

———, *Theban Ostraca; ed. from the Originals*, 1913.

Goedicke, H., "The '400-Years Stela' reconsidered," *Bulletin of the Egyptological Seminar* 3, 1981.

Goedicke, H., ed., *Perspectives on the Battle of Kadesh*, 1985.

Golvin, J.-C., and Goyon, J.-C., *Les Bâtisseurs de Karnak*, 1987.

Grimal, N., *Les Termes de la propagande royale égyptienne, de la XIXe dynastie à la conquête d'Alexandre*, 1986.

Healy, M., *Qadesh 1300 BC: Clash of the Warrior Kings*, 1993.

Lefebvre, G., *Essai sur la médecine égyptienne de l'époque pharaonique*, 1956.

Margueron, J.-C., and Pfirsch, L., *Le Proche-Orient et l'Egypte antiques*, 1996.

Maspéro, G., *Les Momies Royales de Deir el-Bahari*, 1889.

Menu, B., *Le Régime juridique des terres et du personnel attaché à la terre dans le Papyrus Wilbour*, 1970.

———, *L'Obélisque de la Concorde*, 1987.

———, "La Proclamation de l'empire par Aménophis III," *Méditerranées* 5, 1995.

———, "Naissance du pouvoir pharaonique," *Méditerranées* 6/7, 1996

———, "Enseignes et porte-étendards," *Bulletin de l'Institut Français d'Archéologie Orientale* 96, 1996.

———, "L'Emergence et la Symbolique du pouvoir royal, de la palette de Narmer aux textes des Pyramides," *Méditerranées* 13, 1997.

Murnane, W. J., *The Road to Qadesh: A Historical Interpretation of the Battle Reliefs of King Sety I at Karnak*, 1990.

FICTION AND DRAMA ABOUT RAMESSES

Bantock, G., *Rameses II: A Drama of Ancient Egypt*, 1892.

Gedge, P., *House of Illusions: A Novel*, 1997.

———, *Lady of the Reeds*, 1995.

Jacq, C., *La Dame d'Abou Simbel*, 1996.

Lalouette, C., *Memoires de Ramsès le Grand*, 1993.

Tacconi, B., *Ramsete e il sogno di Kadesh*, 1985.

Thiam, A. K., *Ramses II, le nègre: Le théâtre de la grandeur*, 1993.

Chronology

All dates are BC; *dates are approximate and refer to reigns; overlapping dates indicate coregencies.*

PREDYNASTIC PERIOD

Dynasty 0, second half of the 4th millennium

ARCHAIC PERIOD

1st Dynasty, c. 3100–2890
    Narmer (Menes), called the Founder, c. 3100
    Union of Egypt, establishment of the line of pharaohs
2d Dynasty, c. 2890–2682

OLD KINGDOM

3d Dynasty, c. 2686–2613
4th Dynasty, c. 2613–2494
5th Dynasty, c. 2494–2345
6th Dynasty, c. 2345–2181

FIRST INTERMEDIATE PERIOD

7th–8th Dynasties, c. 2181–2125
9th–10th Dynasties, c. 2160–2025

MIDDLE KINGDOM

11th Dynasty, c. 2125–1985
12th Dynasty, c. 1985–1795

SECOND INTERMEDIATE PERIOD

13th Dynasty, c. 1795–1650
14th Dynasty, c. 1750–1650
15th–16th Dynasties (Hyksos), c. 1650–1550
17th Dynasty (princes of Thebes), c. 1650–1550

NEW KINGDOM

18th Dynasty, c. 1550–1295
    Ahmose I, 1550–1525
    Amenhotep I, 1525–1504
    Thutmose I, 1504–1492
    Thutmose II, 1492–1479
    Hatshepsut, 1479–1457
    Thutmose III, 1479–1425
    Amenhotep II, 1427–1400
    Thutmose IV, 1400–1390
    Amenhotep III, 1390–1352
    Akhenaten (Amenhotep IV), 1352–1336
    Neferneferuaten, 1338–1336
    Tutankhamun, 1336–1327

    Ay, 1327–1323
    Horemheb, 1323–1295
19th Dynasty, c. 1295–1186
    Ramesses I, c. 1295–1294
    Seti I, c. 1294–1279
    Ramesses II, called the Great, c. 1279–1213
        Year 1 (c. 1279): Ramesses becomes sole pharaoh
        Year 5 (c. 1274): battle of Qadesh
        Year 17 (c. 1263): proposed date of the biblical Exodus
        Year 18 (c. 1262): Uhri-Teshub, failed pretender to the Hittite throne, flees to Egypt
        Year 21 (c. 1259): Egyptian–Hittite treaty; temples at Abu Simbel probably completed
        Year 25 (c. 1255): Death of Queen Nefertari? (born c. 1300), principal royal wife; Isetnofret becomes chief queen
        Year 30 (c. 1250): first 30-year jubilee
        Year 34 (c. 1246): first Hittite marriage, with Princess Manefrure
        Year 55 (c. 1225): Prince Merenptah named heir
        Year 67 (c. 1213): death of Ramesses
    Merenptah, c. 1213–1203
    Amenmessu, c. 1203–1200
    Seti II, 1200–1194
    Saptah, 1194–1188
    Tausret, 1188–1186
20th Dynasty, c. 1186–1069

THIRD INTERMEDIATE PERIOD

21st Dynasty, c. 1069–945
22d–24th Dynasties (ruling various areas of Egypt), c. 945–715

LATE PERIOD

25th Dynasty (Nubian or Kushite), c. 747–656
26th Dynasty (Saite), 664–525
27th Dynasty (first Persian period), c. 525–404
28th Dynasty, c. 404–399
29th Dynasty, c. 399–380
30th Dynasty, c. 118–106
Second Persian period, 380–343
Macedonian period, 332–305
    Macedonian Conquest (Alexander the Great), 332
    Ptolemaic Dynasty, 305–30
    With the death of Cleopatra, last of the Ptolemies, the Roman Empire comprises Egypt.

List of Illustrations

Index

Photograph Credits

Agence Top 126a–127l. Agence Top/H. Champollion front cover 4, 12, 24r–25l, 43a, 56, 68r, 72a, 95a. Agence Top/Le Diascorn 81r. AKG Photo, Paris 2, 7, 22–23, 106a, 108, 109l. AKG/H Bock 70–71, 148. AKG/Werner Forman back cover, 28a–29l, 29r, 33, 67b, 120b, 130, 132a, 132b. All rights reserved 17b, 37, 53l, 75l, 95b, 97r, 101b, 104l, 109r, 119b, 137, 140, 141. Altitude/Yann Arthus Bertrand 15. P. Barry, courtesy TWA, Inc., 133. Bridgeman-Giraudon 64–65, 112, 116a. Centre National de la Recherche Scientifique/cl. Magali Roux 26b, 27b, 27c. Dagli Orti 8, 26a–27a, 38r–39a, 39b, 39c, 46l, 61r, 72b, 82, 84l, 84r, 90b, 91b, 93, 94a, 97l, 102, 103, 105r, 106b, 107b, 113, 115a, 115b, 117, 118a, 118b, 119a, 120c, 121b, 122b–23b, 124–25, 129. Editions Errance/Jean-Claude Golvin 76–77, 78–79. H. Fontaines, Paris 6, 66b, 66a–67a, 74b–75b, 120a–21a. Editions Gallimard 94b, 96a, 98. Gallimard Jeunesse Archives spine, 11, 40, 88b–89b, 90al, 90ar–91al, 91ar, 92. Giraudon-Bridgeman 122a–23a. Jean-Claude Golvin 5, 58r–59b, 60–61l, 69, 80l, 80r–81l. Kenneth S. Graetz, Montreal 57, 74a, 85. Jürgen Liepe, Berlin 83, 100a–101a, 127r. J.-E. Livet, Paris 14, 45, 46r, 55b, 99, 100b, 110a, 110b–111b, 111a. Magnum/ Bruno Barbey 32. Magnum/Elliot Erwitt 86r–87. Magnum/E. Lessing 3, 16, 25r, 30, 31, 38l, 41, 42, 54b, 62b, 63a, 86l, 96b, 104r–105l. J. Marthelot/Etienne Revault Visuel 19. Ny Carlsberg Glyptotek, Copenhagen 24l. Réunion des Musées Nationaux, Paris 13, 20l, 21a, 34a, 34b, 35, 36, 43b, 44l, 44r, 47a, 52, 53r, 58l, 62a, 63b, 75r, 88a, 89a, 107a, 114, 116b. E. Revault 59a. Rijkmuseum van Oudheden, Leyden 17a. A. Siliotti, Verona 9, 20b–21b, 47b, 48l, 48r–49l, 49r, 50, 51, 54a–55a, 73, 135, 138, 139b, 147. Special Collections, New York Public Library 139a. Sygma 126b, 128.

Text Credits

From *Ancient Egyptian Literature: A Book of Readings,* translated and edited by Miriam Lichtheim, Volume II: *The New Kingdom,* © 1973–1980 Regents of the University of California. From *Echoes of Egyptian Voices: An Anthology of Ancient Egyptian Poetry,* translated and © 1992 by John L. Foster, published by the University of Oklahoma Press. Reprinted by permission of the publishers and the Loeb Classical Library from *Herodotus: The Persian Wars,* volume I, translated by A. D. Godley, Cambridge, Mass., Harvard University Press, 1920, and London, William Heinemann Ltd (Reed Books), reprinted 1975. From *Hymns, Prayers, and Songs: An Anthology of Ancient Egyptian Lyric Poetry, First Harper's Song from the Tomb of Neferhotep [Theban Tomb 50],* translated and © 1995 by John L. Foster, published by Society of Biblical Literature and Scholar's Press. *Pharaoh Triumphant: The Life and Times of Ramesses II, King of Egypt* by K. A. Kitchen, published by Aris & Phillips Ltd., Warminster, England © K. A. Kitchen, 1982. All rights reserved. From *Popular Stories of Ancient Egypt* by Gaston Maspéro, translated by A. S. Johns (University Books, Inc., 1967), by permission of Macmillan Library Reference, New York. From *Diodorus of Sicily,* translated by C. H. Oldfather, published by Harvard University Press, Cambridge, Mass., and London, England, 1933, reprinted 1989.

Bernadette Menu
is Director of Research at the Centre National de
la Recherche Scientifique, Montpellier I. She studied
the history of law and Egyptology at the Faculté des
Lettres in Lille and the Ecole Pratique des Hautes
Etudes, receiving her Ph.D. from the Faculté du
Droit, Paris, with a dissertation on a major fiscal
text dating of the Ramesside period. The most
important of her numerous scientific articles have
been collected in two volumes of *Recherches*. She has
taught Egyptian and Demotic hieroglyphics at the
Université, Lille III and the Institut Catholique,
Paris, and has published a method for learning the
language, a large volume of documents relating to
the Obelisk of Luxor, now at the Place de la
Concorde, Paris, and numerous scholarly articles.
She is a laureate of the Academie Française.

*For Jean-Christophe, Séraphine, Ophélie, Raphaëlle,
and Pol-Eliott, whose* beau nom *is Théophile*

Copyright © Gallimard 1998

English translation © Harry N. Abrams, Inc.,
New York, 1999

First published in Great Britain in 1999 by
Thames and Hudson Ltd, London

Translated by Laurel Hirsch

British Library Cataloguing-in-Publication Data

A catalogue record for this book is available from
the British Library

ISBN 0–500–30089–5

Printed and bound in Italy
by Editoriale Lloyd, Trieste